Submarine Torbay

PAUL CHAPMAN

ROBERT HALE · LONDON

© Paul Chapman 1989
First published in Great Britain 1989

Robert Hale Limited
Clerkenwell House
Clerkenwell Green
London EC1R 0HT

British Library Cataloguing in Publication Data

Chapman, Paul
Submarine Torbay.
1. World War 2. Naval operations during Mediterranean
campaign. Great Britain. Royal navy submarines.
Torbay. Biographies
I. Title
940.54'51'0924

ISBN 0–7090–3821–6

Set in Palatino by
Derek Doyle & Associates, Mold, Clwyd.
Printed in Great Britain by
St Edmundsbury Press, Bury St Edmunds, Suffolk,
bound by WBC Bookbinders Ltd.

Contents

Illustrations

Maps

Foreword

by Vice-Admiral Sir Hugh Mackenzie
KCB,DSO*,DSC

When I joined my first submarine as a junior officer in 1935 the first lieutenant was Lieutenant A.C.C.Miers; he already had a reputation throughout the submarine service for resolute, bold, determined and decisive action, and great honesty of purpose, whether on duty or off; I quickly learned that whatever one attempted one had to follow strictly the appropriate 'rules of the game' – nothing else was acceptable. Our friendship lasted until his death in 1985. I was fortunate to be a fellow Commanding Officer in the same submarine flotilla in the Mediterranean in 1941 and 1942, and again with him in the submarine flotilla of which he was then 'Commander S/M' in the south-west Pacific in 1944/45. I thus feel particularly privileged to write this foreword to *Submarine Torbay*, an epic story of a dedicated ship's company, which presents so fully the unique character and remarkable personality of the man who led them.

This very human yet factual account of HMS *Torbay's* exploits in her first commission (1940–42) is greatly to be welcomed. It is very fitting that the truth of her record be published and become widely known, especially for two specific reasons: first, lest with the passage of time the full horrors and dangers of all-out conventional war cease to be recognized – or the demands it makes on those directly involved; and secondly, and just as importantly, to set the record straight; particularly is this so in view of the unjustified posthumous defamation of her Commanding

Officer recently carried by certain elements of the national press.

For those of us, now old men, who served in submarines in the Mediterranean during World War II, and particularly throughout that phase of it covered by this book, our memories are almost inevitably dimmed and we will have forgotten much of what was endured and, through that endurance, what was achieved. Read the book, however, and our memories are vividly refreshed and it is all brought back to mind so clearly.

To the younger generation who had not our experience it presents a true and striking record which cannot fail but illuminate their understanding of submarine operations, the successes, the trials, the tribulations at that time – so critical to the outcome of the North African campaign and the eventual winning of the war.

Above all it is a tribute to the courage, determination and endurance of the ship's company of HMS *Torbay*, under the leadership of a Commanding Officer imbued with an exceptional sense of duty and of service to the Royal Navy and to his country, with that offensive spirit so essential to victory in war, yet withal deeply conscious of the continued well-being of all under his command.

H.S.M.
Sylvan Lodge, Puttenham.
April 1989

1 Introduction

In which the author introduces Torbay *and her 1941
crew and describes her capabilities and shortcomings*

Late in 1940 the submarine *Torbay* was being completed in
Chatham Dockyard where she had been built; she sailed
for trials and working up in January 1941.

At this time the British were 'alone', though not really.
As Churchill said, 'Alone, but up-borne by every generous
heart-beat of mankind.' He could not have been thinking
of the Soviet Union. They had helped the Axis with
supplies during the elimination of Poland, Norway,
Denmark, the Netherlands, Belgium, France, Yugoslavia
and Greece. Also Ribbentrop and Molotov were discussing the methodology of carving up the British Empire. In
due course first Soviet Communists and then German
Nazis got what they so richly deserved. This is perhaps
water under the bridge, but the student of history should
not ignore the facts.

Alone? Canadians were in England, Australians and
Indians were in the Middle East and East Africa. New
Zealanders, South Africans and Rhodesians were on the
way or already there to defend the Empire's pivot in the
Middle East and Persian Gulf. In the United States the
Lend-Lease Bill, without which it is hard to imagine how
we could have survived, was going through Congress.

To the thoughtful, it seemed clear that we could survive.
After all, the Luftwaffe had failed to destroy the Royal Air
Force. The German Army, that most formidable proposi-

tion, simply did not have equipment and supporting forces to cross the Channel with hope of success. So far, so good, but how were we going to win?

The point may be illustrated by a conversation with a Norwegian submarine officer. We were walking, on a beautiful 1940 autumn afternoon, on the Isle of Mull in the Western Isles. Said I: 'My sense of history tells me that we will win, but I have to admit that I do not see how.' Said he: 'I do not know either, but of course we win; that is why I came from Norway.' He was killed three years later, so he did not live to see his vision here; but I expect he heard the news in Heaven.

In the Mediterranean and the Middle East, which was *Torbay's* scene, the British were hanging on by their eyelids. We held Gibraltar, but Hitler had a plan 'Felix', to come down through Spain and take it. We held Malta, but this was in effect knocked out as an operational base in the early months of 1942; moreover, the Axis had a plan to capture the island. In the Western Desert the arrival of Rommel's Afrika Korps was to nullify Wavell's late 1940 defeat of the Italians. Thus our tenure even of Egypt and the Suez Canal was precarious.

In mid and late 1941 respectively the Soviet Union and the United States became ranged against the Axis powers, so at the end of *Torbay's* first commission, in mid 1942, the picture was quite different. Hard disasters were still to come – for example, the fall of Tobruk – but to the student of history victory was simply a matter of time, provided only that our determination did not falter.

Anthony Miers' determination did not falter. He was the commanding officer of *Torbay*, throughout her first commission.

This is perhaps the place to say something about *Torbay's* people.

We start with the late Sir Anthony Miers VC,KBE,CB,DSO & Bar. He was the captain, and as such was 'Sir', and at the end of the first commission he had the VC and the DSO & Bar. The other honours came later and included a United States decoration. At the start he was plain

Lieutenant-Commander Miers; by the end of 1941 he had become Commander Miers.

For a number of reasons, those who sailed in *Torbay* from Chatham, in January 1941, were by no means the same as those who sailed for the Bay of Biscay, and thence to the Mediterranean, on 22 March 1941. *Torbay* sailed at fifteen hours notice; half the crew and three of the five officers had just gone on leave, from the Holy Loch in the Clyde, towards London and beyond. When the message came, they were passing Carlisle on their way south; it was certain that none of them could be recalled in time. So, the most junior officer moved up to first lieutenant, which is also second in command. Three more officers were obtained or borrowed, and the missing half-crew was replaced from depot ship spare crew. There were a number of changes in the fifteen months following; but these were minor by comparison.

Members of the crew came from Scotland (including Orkney), England (all parts), Wales, Ulster, Eire and New Zealand. A better-natured and more enthusiastic body of men it would be hard to find.

The functions of the leading members of the crew of some sixty of the T-class submarine may be briefly explained.

The captain had overall responsibility, and in particular for the tactical operation of the boat, such as what sort of targets should be attacked, and with what; for example, torpedo, gun, demolition charge. The captain's patrol orders might set certain limits, such as, if lying in wait for the *Scharnhorst* and *Gneisenau*, leave all else alone. The captain's disciplinary powers, when at sea or on detached duty, were draconian; whereas if the submarine was in the presence of higher authority in harbour, the serious matters would be referred up, probably with recommendation as to the penalty to be imposed.

The first lieutenant was responsible to the captain for discipline, for the boat's working routine, for electrics and for trimming; that is, adjusting ballast water as necessary to maintain correct buoyancy condition. To assist the first lieutenant were a coxswain, a chief petty officer and chief 'policeman'; a second coxswain, an electrical artificer for the low-power (20 volt) systems; a petty officer leading torpedo operator for main motors, main batteries and high-power (240 volt) systems. In those days the torpedo branch also covered electrics; nowadays electrics is a separate branch. A chief stoker petty officer assisted by carrying out, and advising on, the necessary major ballast water adjustments. When the submarine was submerged, however, minor ballast adjustments tended to be a continuing process carried out by the officer of the watch, whoever he might be.

The engineer officer looked after the hull, the main (diesel) engines and all auxiliary machinery and systems. He was assisted by a chief engine-room artificer, an outside engine-room artificer (for all machinery outside the engine-room), two other engine-room artificers, the chief stoker petty officer, one or more stoker petty officers and, of course, stokers.

The 'third hand' was a seaman lieutenant or sub-lieutenant and usually had charge of torpedoes, assisted by a petty officer torpedo gunner's mate, and of the gun, assisted by a leading or able seaman gunlayer. The third hand might also be correspondence officer.

The 'fourth hand' was a seaman lieutenant or sub-lieutenant responsible for navigation, Asdics (Sonar) and signals (radio or visual). There would be a petty officer or leading seaman (higher submarine detector) for Asdics; for signals there would be a petty officer telegraphist plus three telegraphists and a leading signalman for the visual side and for message distribution.

The third and fourth hands were, in fact, more or less interchangeable, and appointment changes could result in third and fourth duties being the other way round.

Some of the crew were experienced submariners, others were not. For example, Miers had thirteen years experience against his first lieutenant's nine months. On the other hand, the first lieutenant was the only officer who had been on submarine patrols in war, whereas Miers had been on the staff of the Commander-in-Chief Home Fleet. None of the officers, and few of the crew, had ever heard a depth-charge fired in anger. They did not have long to wait.

The early submarines were called 'submarine boats'. Thus submarines were colloquially known as 'boats' rather than 'ships'. From the shore base, or from the submarine depot ship, you went 'down the boat'.

What sort of a boat was *Torbay*? She was of the largest size under construction at the start of World War II. Some earlier classes of submarine were larger – for example, the River, 'O', 'P', 'R' and minelayer classes. *Torbay* was formidably armed: she had ten 21-inch torpedo tubes, all facing forward; six tubes were internal, and four external to the pressure hull. The six internal tubes had reload torpedoes ranged behind them; the four externals could not be reloaded except back at base. Even so, this meant an initial salvo of up to ten, followed by a further salvo of at least six. The torpedoes were not of the 'intelligent' breed which is commonplace nowadays; they were straight runners, and you pointed the submarine in the direction in which you wished them to go. There was, in fact, a primitive form of torpedo angling, but I never heard of its being used; it was difficult or even impracticable to keep the angling system free from gross error.

Torbay also had a 4-inch quick-firing gun. The 'quick firing' was achieved by human skill and drill, not by mechanical means. Those who have seen the field-gun competition at the Royal Tournament will have seen the sort of teamwork required. There were also small arms such as bren-guns, rifles and revolvers. The gunnery armament played a large part in the *Torbay* story, not least in shooting up an aircraft on the ground.

Torbay did not have the very high speed and almost unlimited endurance of modern nuclear-propelled submarines. She could do 14 knots on the surface, and 9 knots submerged, but the latter only for about an hour before her batteries were exhausted. Battery power was the Achilles heel, closely followed by high-pressure air. Air was needed for blowing ballast tanks, firing torpedoes and domestic services. The air compressors, which recharged

the air bottles, ran on electricity from the batteries. The first
lieutenant, as the captain's 'housekeeper', would sometimes be faced with a dilemma: which element, battery or
high-pressure air, needed replenishment first. To get this
right, he had to measure what had happened and then to
guess what was likely to happen in the next few hours.

A paramount factor was that *Torbay* had to come to the
surface, and to remain there for some hours, usually by
night but by day if opportunity offered, to recharge batteries and air. Surfacing was also necessary to refresh the
atmosphere, otherwise, with almost sixty men breathing in
a confined space, dangerous levels of carbon dioxide would
build up. On the surface the diesel engines could be used,
but in those days there was no such thing as a snort mast to
allow diesel engines to be run when submerged.

In those days, nothing like as much as of now was known
about carbon dioxide (CO_2) poisoning. The problem comes
through very clearly from study of a book *The Admiralty
Regrets ...* by Warren and Benson. * This tells the story of the
sinking, following an accident, of the submarine *Thetis* in
Liverpool Bay in June 1939. Four only out of the 103 on
board managed to escape, using Davis submerged escape
apparatus; from the evidence of Leading Stoker Arnold,
one of the second pair to get out, most of those onboard had
become incapacitated by CO_2 poisoning. *Thetis* was raised,
refitted and renamed *Thunderbolt*. Her captain, Cecil Ber-
nard Crouch, won three DSOs before *Thunderbolt* met her
end, in March 1943, at the hands of the Italian sloop *Cicogna*
(Capitano di Corvetta Augusto Migliorini), near Trapani in
Sicily. From Migliorini's evidence, it is clear that CO_2
poisoning was the reason for *Thunderbolt*'s loss.

This is what happens. The first onset of the poisoning
induces a light-headed, giggly feeling; everything is so
bloody funny. If this condition is not recognized for what
it is, and something is not done about it, trouble follows,
because the next stage is a 'couldn't care less' lassitude.
Death will come when the concentration reaches about
ten per cent, but to some it may come earlier. From

* Odhams Press; The Popular Book Club, 1958.

Migliorini's story, it seems that *Thunderbolt* had been dived for about twenty-nine hours and was in the 'couldn't care less' condition.

Fuel was never a problem in the Mediterranean; it is only some 2,000 miles from Gibraltar to Alexandria; we had enough fuel to go from end to end five times.

It so happened that William of Orange, when he came to England in 1688 to take up the throne with his wife Mary, landed at Torbay in Devonshire. Thus HMS *Torbay* was given as badge a bugle from William's coat of arms. Also *Torbay* was given William's motto, *'Je maintiendrai'*.

The bugle was splendid, but Tony Miers did not care for the motto. It sounded to him too much like 'I will get back to harbour'; he thought that something more adventurous would be appropriate. So he went to the Admiralty and persuaded them to change the motto to *'Penetrabo'* ('I will get in'). Certainly the new motto was more in keeping with what was to happen. Nor was this just in her first commission: *Torbay* distinguished herself in two later ones; not many submarines survived to complete three. If these later commissions are to be chronicled, it should not be by this author, because he was not there.

This account derives from Tony Miers official reports, by courtesy of the Public Record Office. In addition there are personal memories, and accounts from old friends, which would not feature in formal reports.

2 Some Operational Considerations

A description of equipment, techniques and tactics of the time

The *Torbay* story will include many such events as being attacked with depth-charges, sightings of hostile aircraft and sightings of hostile surface craft. To follow the story clearly, one must understand some of the limitations both of the equipment and of the techniques available at the time.

Depth-charges were a kind of scatter-gun weapon. They were dropped at intervals, over the stern; and perhaps a 'pattern' of depth-charges would be filled out, in the horizontal plane, by charges fired sideways from a patrol vessel's after deck. Usually the attacker would not know exactly where the submarine was, or its precise depth, so the best that could be done was to plaster the suspect area in both horizontal and vertical planes. Depth-charges were a long way removed from the precision weapons of the 1980s; even so, they could sink, damage or miss a submarine.

Hostile aircraft had no radar, so they were not much of a menace at night. They had no listener-buoys to drop, like the modern sonobuoys which are dropped into the sea and monitored in the aircraft. The aircraft might have only bombs, and no depth-charges, in which case they tended to be lethal only against surfaced submarines. Even so, the submarine *Thrasher*, caught while still fairly close to the surface, found that she was carrying two unexploded bombs. When she surfaced at night, one was on and the other inside the forward casing. The first lieutenant and the second coxswain managed to get rid of them overboard. Lieutenant Roberts and Petty Officer Gould both got Victoria Crosses.

The mere presence of hostile aircraft could prevent a submarine from using its surface mobility, by day at any rate, to gain an attacking position. Moreover, in the then clear waters of the Mediterranean (before today's pollution) a submarine might be visible, from an aircraft, even when down at a keel-depth of 100 feet. But this would be so only if the aircraft was actually overhead, or nearly so, and if its crew had the time and keenness to be looking down at the right moment. An aircraft would not see a deep submarine from an oblique position, unless the submarine were to be making a surface disturbance, in which case the submarine would be guilty of bad housekeeping.

The sighting of hostile aircraft could actually help a submarine. An important ship or convoy would usually have an air as well as a surface escort. The first indication that something was coming might well be a Cant or Macchi aircraft patrolling ahead. Soon after, smoke might be sighted, then masts, then funnels and finally the ships themselves. The aircraft's movements would have indicated the general line of advance.

Enemy surface craft, at the time, were using hydrophones to detect submarines. Hydrophones are listeners only. If a submarine could keep very quiet (for example, by no use of high speed, no use of noisy auxiliary machinery, no noisy blowing of ballast tanks), hydrophones might be largely ineffective. Later on in *Torbay*'s first commission enemy surface craft started to use active Sonar, then called Asdic. However, this was in their hands such a new toy that its tactical use tended to be inexpert.

Both Sonar and hydrophones were affected by water conditions. In some places in the Mediterranean, particularly in summer, there would be a layer of warmer water sitting upon a cooler layer. Again, in other places, and most markedly at such places as the approaches to the Dardanelles, there would be a layer of cooler, fresher water sitting upon water of greater salinity. These layers could have quite different densities.

These layer conditions caused problems for both surface craft and submarines. Layers affected the travel of sound waves in much the same way as a straight stick, half in air and half in water, seems to the eye to be bent. The layers also caused problems to what submarines call 'trim'. Trim, or 'balance' is the same as an aircraft's trim. Ideally, dived submarines should be neutrally buoyant; that is, they should be exactly the same weight as the water displaced. Then, if a submarine stops, she remains where she is in the vertical plane; otherwise, either she sinks or she rises to the surface.

Major adjustments to trim are made by adding (flooding) or subtracting (pumping) sea water from auxiliary ballast tanks. Flooding is fast; pumping is slow; and the faster and the slower the deeper the submarine is. Fine adjustments are made by hydroplanes. These are like fish fins, and depend for their effectiveness upon the fact that the submarine is moving through the water, even if slowly; if the submarine is moving fast, hydroplanes can correct for a considerable imbalance. The ideal situation is for a submarine to be neutrally buoyant but to be trimmed so that she is pointing slightly down, a state known as 'bubble aft'. Then, if required, the hydroplanes can steer her down with no extra flooding of ballast or increase in speed.

Both layers and water pressure complicate the equation. If a submarine goes from a layer of one density to one of another, she is at once not in trim, and pumping or flooding must be undertaken. Water pressure has a different effect. It increases by roughly one pound per square inch per two feet of keel-depth. When a submarine goes deep, the frames on which the skin or hull is built will stand the strain, up to the point of total collapse. The steel plates between the frames, however, will be distorted slightly inwards. Then the submarine will be displacing marginally less water and so will become heavy in relation to her environment. Normally a submarine going deep must pump to maintain trim, and vice versa, but layers may make the converse appropriate.

At the time, neither enemy surface craft nor British submarines had warning surface radar, so that at night they had either to see or to hear each other. Submarine Sonar was relatively primitive, so that the best 'sensor' was still the Mark 1 Eyeball. The submariner, when submerged, had to use the eyeball through a periscope; but periscopes were not very long, so that, when the submerged submarine could see, it could also be rammed by patrol craft except those of the shallowest draught.

For a submarine, a crippling limitation was lack of mobility. In that context, World War II submarines have been described as 'slightly intelligent mines'. They could travel submerged some nine miles in an hour but after that they had to creep about, at 2 knots or less, until opportunity arose to recharge exhausted batteries. During this operation, which took several hours, they were a bit like sitting ducks; they could only dive out of the way to the further detriment of their batteries. This meant that, if you had chosen a bad position in which to dive at dawn, there was little chance of doing something useful during the following day. Submarines were thus aptly described as 'weapons of position and surprise'. If the submarine's position was known, surprise was lost and, except in such cases as focal points off harbour entrances, the position could be skirted round. Hence the importance of not transmitting on radio unless it was intended drastically to change position soon after. Having said this, there were occasions when the submarine wanted to 'trail its coat' and let it be known that it was around somewhere. One such occasion is described in Chapter 5, *Torbay*'s second patrol.

Nowadays submarines do not have guns; guns detract from streamlining and from quiet underwater performance; submarines have torpedoes and missiles. But in World Wars I and II the submarine gun was a most potent weapon; see the Jolly Rogers of *Triumph* and *Torbay* in the Jolly Roger montage; each star indicates a successful action with the gun.

The elderly 'O'-, 'P'- and 'R'-class submarines and the minelaying submarines like *Rorqual* and the 'T'-class were particularly suited to this form of aggression. For a start, they had the heavier punch of a 4-inch calibre gun, as against the 3-inch calibre of the 'S' and 'U' classes. More important, the gun was in what may be called an open-topped turret, as opposed to the 'S' and 'U' classes which had a 'naked' gun on the casing just in front of the conning tower.

Also important was that the larger submarines had double upper gun tower hatches leading to the gun; the 'S' class had just one; the 'U' class had no gun tower at all, so that the gun's crew had to scramble over the front of the bridge to get to the gun. All the foregoing considerations had a bearing on the speed of getting the gun into action, and the damage it could cause when it did. Speed and damage, thus quickly putting the enemy into a state of disarray, were the secret of success.

These would be the tactics: stalk the enemy from submerged to a position abaft his beam, and at a range of 1,000 yards or less; then surface, at the rush, and open fire. If there was not already a pressure well above atmospheric in the submarine, air would be released from the high-pressure air bottles to make sure that there was; then the hatches, both conning tower and gun tower, could be opened when they were still a little under water; the rush of air escaping would blow the water away. With any luck to go with good judgement, the enemy would be being hit before they realized where the trouble was coming from; look-outs tend to look out ahead rather than behind them. (That was why *Torbay* used four look-outs, each with his own 90-degree sector; and they were not allowed to look at what was going on in somebody else's sector, however interesting or exciting that might be.)

Naturally, at the sort of close and decisive range described, the submarine would be open to return fire from small arms such as machine-guns, which could come into action very fast. The bigger submarines, with their gun in an open-topped turret, would have their gun's crew almost entirely under protection, as opposed to standing in full view around the naked gun of the 'S' and 'U' classes. Thus the larger submarines were better placed to take liberties with the gun.

A statistic, which the writer has heard but is not in a position to authenticate, affirms, that, 'British submarines sank more, by gunfire alone, than the rest of the Royal Navy put together.' It sounds highly improbable, but underline *'by gunfire alone'*. One remembers that very large targets, like the *Bismarck* and the *Scharnhorst*, though pounded into a helpless state by the cannonades of battleships, were eventually sunk by torpedoes. Well, it has been said, 'There are lies, damned lies and statistics.' Even so, this particular statistic is quite plausible.

Submarines used their guns quite often in the shore bombardment role. *Torbay* did the aircraft hangar, and the aircraft on the ground, as told in Chapter 9. Opposition from shore batteries was a possibility, or a certainty, depending on the locality. But consider the enemy's problem: he would never have enough personnel to keep full guns' crews closed up all the time, so it would take him at least minutes to get into action unless there had been prior warning. A submarine, appearing literally 'out of the blue' and disappearing when it has had enough, is a difficult thing with which to cope. During the minutes that the shore battery takes to get going, a well-drilled submarine gun's crew should be popping off at ten rounds per minute. In the writer's experience of seven shore bombardments in *Torbay* and in *Upstart*, the enemy's reply delay ranged from four to fifteen minutes. This last did not do the enemy much good, because by that time *Upstart* was off, having expended all her ammunition.

The submarine gun was used not only in the Mediterranean; it was used in the North Sea in the opening phase of World War II and extensively in the Far East in the later phases.

Whilst there were 'Special Operations', the main operational need was simple and vital. It was to inhibit reinforcement and supplies reaching the German and Italian Armies in North Africa and Crete. Their supply routes from Europe were the relatively short runs from Italy, Yugoslavia and Greece.

On the other hand, the variously called Commonwealth 'Army of the Nile', 'Desert Army' or 'Eighth Army' depended upon supply from the Persian Gulf, South Africa, India the United Kingdom and the United States. Troops and supplies, such as replacement aircraft, could come across from West Africa by air; but the vast preponderance came by sea, by very long haul.

Enemy signal traffic was being read and understood by the Intelligence services. Rommel's bleats about shortage of supply were incessant. So it seemed that the assault upon his communications by aircraft, surface ships and submarines was hurting; in fact, Rommel's final advance was made possible only by the immense booty he captured at Tobruk in mid 1942.

As we know, Rommel's final advance was stemmed by Auchinleck in the battles around the El Alamein lines, was rebuffed by Montgomery at Alam Halfa and was routed by Montgomery at El Alamein in the autumn of 1942. *Torbay* was not in on this kill; she was due a refit and reached home in early June 1942.

3 Chatham to the Clyde

Torbay's trials and Chapman's tribulations

For Lieutenant Chapman, the beginning was in the Clyde, where the small, 1917 vintage submarine *H 34* was working at training exercises for anti-submarine vessels at Campbeltown, Tobermory, with one stint at Scapa Flow.

Soon after Christmas 1940, *H 34* went from the Clyde to Sheerness, where she was due to refit. At her best 8½ knots, the trip took some time, but she arrived safely on 7 January 1941 at dusk. Chapman had been looking forward to refit; it might give him the chance to see something of the wife he had married a month before. However, as soon as the picking-up rope was secured to the buoy, the signal tower started to wink. Signalman Roberts called out the message as he read it: '*H 34* from Admiral Submarines: Lieutenant Chapman is to be lent to *Torbay* at Chatham, date to be reported.'

Next morning, after turning over navigation to the first lieutenant, and signal and confidential books to the captain, Chapman caught the trot boat up river to Chatham. There he found *Torbay*, still completing. There he met, for the first time, Lieutenant-Commander Tony Miers, Paul Skelton as first lieutenant, Leo Wood as chief engineer, and 'Knocker' as third hand. Chapman became fourth hand; that is, he had charge of navigation, signal and confidential books, and correspondence. The story was that the previous fourth hand had gone sick and was not likely to return before it was time to sail. The truth was – in

Chapman's interest, lest it should upset him – suppressed. It was that Miers had summarily administered the sack. Nor was this destined to be the only such occasion.

Chapman had much to do getting charts up to date and plotting thereon the latest information about minefields. It seemed that his predecessor had not bothered with such detail. It occupied the time until *Torbay* was almost ready to set forth.

Before sailing from Chatham, there was a briefing by the staff of the Commander-in-Chief, the Nore. All our officers were there to absorb what particularly affected each. A Commander Linzee was the principal speaker. He told us the routes we were to follow, up the east coast and then round the top of Scotland and down to the Clyde. He told us when we were to tack on behind convoy, when we should meet our own separate escort vessel, and so on.

Then he outlined various administrative matters, such as what reports were required from us, to whom and when, and what signal publications and recognition documents we should carry. Recognition signals were an important element in the avoidance of sad mishaps. One submarine looks very much like another, particularly in the dark, and there were quite a lot of trigger-happy ships and aircraft around. Suffice to say that, a little later, one of our U-class submarines was rammed and sunk, with heavy loss of life, off the east coast, by one of the escorts of a convoy. Before that, a British submarine had torpedoed and sank another British submarine in the North Sea. Later Coastal Command sank a British U-class in the Bay of Biscay.

Chapman pricked up his ears at the recognition documents item. It was wrong, completely wrong. But he had said it, and that was what they would give us unless something was done fast. Chapman looked across the room at Miers but he was showing no reaction. Thus Chapman rose. He was still wearing sub-lieutenant's uniform, because there had been time to get the second stripe only on the best suit. He told the commander, politely, that he was in error, and why; then he added what should have been said. This would not have happened in the nineteenth century, and probably not in World War I, because to contradict a senior officer could verge on mutiny.

After a slightly embarrassing silence, Miers rose. Said he, 'It seems there is doubt. Should not you, Commander, and I, go and telephone to Flag Officer Submarines' Headquarters and get a ruling?'

So they went. Our chief engineer, who also doubled as cipher officer and thus had knowledge of secret and confidential books, gave his opinion that Chapman's version must be a mistake. Chapman said nothing. If you know that you know, you may make friends by not rubbing things in. Back came the commander and Tony Miers. Said the commander, 'The sub-lieutenant is quite right. We did not know. Thank you.'

The commander was a good and forthright man. The implications of what had happened were not lost on Miers nor on Chapman, who knew that he could expect support when needed.

After such trials as could be carried out in the restricted, shallow and mined waters of the Thames Estuary, *Torbay* went, northabout, to the Clyde. During the passage, Miers had opportunity to appraise his officers doing some of their duties, though not the whole range, at sea. The third hand was found wanting and was replaced when we reached the Holy Loch in the Clyde. The replacement was senior to Chapman, who thus remained as fourth hand. At the same time, Miers made it clear to Chapman that he was no longer 'on loan'; whether he was ever formally re-appointed is not remembered, nor does it matter.

The trials in the Thames Estuary had included one called 'gun functioning trial'. You did not have to shoot at a target, you had just to fire practice projectiles from the gun at various elevations, to make sure that the gun recoil and recuperation systems were in proper order. The whole estuary was shrouded in low cloud and mist; the trials officer said that we must cancel, because we could not be sure that the range was clear. But Miers was determined not to be set back a day.

Chapman, from the chart, gave Miers a safe bearing on which to fire, so that the shots would fall on shallow water rather than on land. Admittedly there was the very slight chance that a fishing boat could be in the way, nothing bigger because the water was too shallow. Miers ordered the trial to proceed.

Said the trials officer, 'But if the gun does not work properly, you might hit Margate.'

Said Miers, 'Then they will think it an unexploded bomb.'

There was an exercise area reasonably close to the Holy Loch, but nearer still was the deep water of Loch Long in which an individual underwater exercise could be carried out. The southerly part of this loch was a convoy-assembly anchorage. As we found to our cost, if the anchorage was congested, ships were apt to spread over into the northern or exercise area part.

Torbay was proceeding submerged near the south limit when a merchant ship came up, turned to starboard and anchored right in our path. Miers went deep under her and resumed periscope depth between her and the next in the anchorage. This happened to be a small tanker. He ordered that the motors be stopped, and to surface. He then handed the periscope to Chapman and went up the conning tower to be ready to open the hatch. The motors were stopped, but it did not follow that *Torbay* was. Chapman had to readjust the periscope eyepieces, as his settings were not the same as those of Miers.

When this had been done, he did not like what he saw. He ordered full speed astern. When he reached the bridge, Miers had the same idea, but it was already happening. Even so, our knife-edged net-cutter made a nasty slit, above and below water, in the tanker's midships. *Torbay* on the other hand backed off undamaged.

It was rather unusual to pre-empt the commanding officer in this way; but there was just no time to offer advice. Miers' comment was to commend initiative and judgement.

Astonishingly, the tanker had to be beached, lest she sink. We had reservations about this; as later events were to show, it is not all that easy to sink a tanker. Possibilities include that their best people were on shore and the rest did not know what to do; equally, they may have thought, 'Good oh, we have a "Blighty" wound', and did not do too much about it.

When *Torbay* got back alongside the depot ship in the Holy Loch, Miers went inboard to give an account of himself. The other officers, in sombre mood, gathered round a bottle of Plymouth gin in the submarine wardroom. A collision is not a good thing to have; somebody must be at fault, and you can hardly blame it on a ship at anchor. Besides, such things as chart of the scene and the control-room log might be summoned.

Presently First Lieutenant Skelton said, 'Poor old skipper, this will finish him.' Said Chapman, 'You think so?'

'Yes.'

'Then I also am at risk because, at least *de facto*, I was officer of the watch at the time of the collision.'

'I had not thought of that, but so you were.'

Next day the flotilla navigating officer came out in *Torbay* to visit the scene of the crime, and himself to evaluate the problems. The powers-that-were decided to raise no charges, which could have been 'hazarding the ship'. Even so, just a little more delay, measured in seconds, in ordering full speed astern, and *Torbay* would have crumpled her front part in a way that would have taken her back to builders or another dockyard; and with possible unpleasant consequences for Miers and for Chapman.

Although there was no official retribution, a penalty was exacted; it took the form of ribbing, or teasing, of which one example follows. Some days later, *Torbay* was at anchor off Arrochar at the head of Loch Long. Miers and the third hand were at the torpedo range, discussing arrangements for torpedo-discharge trials with Lieutenant-Commanders de Labalmondière and Didham.

Lieutenant-Commander H.F. ('Boggy') Bone called and was received by First Lieutenant Skelton and Navigator Chapman. 'Boggy' was probably on his way to a day out at Loch Lomond; he was the brilliantly successful captain of the submarine *Tigris*, and a most sociable person; he was fresh from a patrol in the Bay of Biscay, where he had clobbered a blockade-running tanker. Paul Skelton ventured to congratulate on the tanker. That gave 'Boggy' his cue to say, 'But I came to congratulate you on yours.'

'Boggy' was to be met some eighteen months later, when

Chapman was doing the submarine commanding officers qualifying course, known as 'The Perisher'. 'Boggy' was the teacher, and the interesting group was: Michael Sars from Norway, Andre Klopotovski from Poland, and from the UK Tony Duff, Toby Weston, 'Flash' Gordon, Bobbie Lambert and Paul Chapman. I believe that all approached the course with some apprehension at having to go through our paces under the eye of one with such an outstanding reputation for efficiency. However, 'Boggy's' patience and wise counsel were such that soon he was no longer feared; he was loved.

In the inter-World War years Asdic, now called Sonar, had become the primary anti-submarine detection device in the Royal Navy. Asdic had then a minor application in the passive or listening role, but it was primarily designed to transmit an underwater signal and to receive an echo from a submerged object.

It resulted that Royal Navy submarine design paid insufficient attention to the problem of self-generated noise. Since the enemies in World War II were, at the outset, still using hydrophones, very efficient listeners at that, this was a serious failing. Experience soon drew attention to the problem.

Torbay was lucky in that her construction incorporated such things as flexible rubber mountings for auxiliary machinery. These machines might otherwise have set up unwanted resonance and reverberations through the pressure hull. Thence, through the sea, noises could reach enemy hydrophones. After completion of normal trials and working up, *Torbay* was ordered to carry out noise trials in the upper reaches of Loch Long. The mind boggles at the primitive arrangements, ludicrous in comparison with the sophisticated noise range set up in Loch Goil some time later. *Torbay* was given some dedicated boffins, led by a Dr Beatty, with a dunking hydrophone and noise-measuring gear, a motor boat and a metre base optical rangefinder.

This was the way of it. We had to wait for outside interference to die away. This interference could be ferries, fishing boats, ships arriving in the southern reaches of

Loch Long, and so on. Thus almost all the work was done late at night in February or March.

Off went the motor boat with boffins and hydrophone, accompanied by Chapman with rangefinder and signal lamp. It was Chapman's business to get the motor boat to the prescribed distance from the submarine, and anchor it. Then the boffins set up their gear, and Chapman signalled the submarine to start the trials. Auxiliary machinery was run, for noise measurement, in a predetermined order. But, to be sure that we knew to what we were listening, Chapman gave a start and stop signal for each machine.

Dr Beatty's team included a Mr Gillette, whose business was resilient mountings. He would closely inspect any machine which seemed to be unexpectedly noisy. The fact that the machine was on resilient mountings meant that, when in operation, it might tremble or wobble; in so doing, it could impinge against fixed piping, or even a bulkhead, and thence transmit noise which the resilient mounts were designed to inhibit. It was practicable sometimes to reposition the object impinged upon, or, if not, to pad it.

There must have been considerable inaccuracies and approximations. For example, the metre base optical rangefinder gets progressively less accurate with range, even more so when both windows keep filling with frozen snow that has to be scraped out with numb fingers. Even so, the results were of great value to *Torbay*, and no doubt to others too.

We found, for example, that our ballast pumps were much noisier than we had imagined. But the horse laugh related to the telemotor system. This system was served by two pumps, a Vickers 'silent' pump, which made the claim indicated, and an Imo pump, which made no such claim. The Vickers 'silent' pump was, in fact, rather noisy, and the Imo was astonishingly quiet.

When *Torbay* was with the depot ship, or at a shore base, there were arrangements for such as Roman Catholics and Anglicans to go to separate venues of worships on Sundays or Holy Days of Obligation. But when *Torbay* was detached, on her own, there might well be no such possibility.

Miers himself was a Roman Catholic. It was customary to order 'Fall out the Roman Catholics' before holding prayers, but he did not intend to absent himself. He advised the ship's company as follows: We all worshipped the same God; therefore we would do it all together, regardless of denomination. He would delegate to the first lieutenant, as the senior representative of the Church attended by the King, to devise a form of worship acceptable to all. Of course, Miers did not ask permission to do this, because he knew that, in those days, he would never get it. He merely anticipated Vatican II by about thirty years. He did tend to be ahead of events.

Following completion of trials and exercises, including the noise trials, *Torbay* was poised for operational service. Instead, she was ordered to take passage to Halifax, Nova Scotia, on 6 March. The idea of going to Halifax was that Atlantic convoys then might have a battleship, or a submarine, included in the escort. The battleship was all very well; she could see off a pocket battleship or disguised merchant vessel raider and could at least cause the *Scharnhorst* and *Gneisenau* to haul off. On the other hand, the chances of a World War II submarine getting into a position to do anything useful were slim. Even so, the thought, no doubt reported by Focke Wulf reconnaissance, that there was a submarine around, would give at least pause for thought to the enemy surface ships.

March 6 happened to be Chapman's twenty-first birthday. In the circumstances, Miers allowed him ashore on the evening of 5 March. This was the better to say '*au revoir*' to his wife of less than three months. She had been in bed, in an hotel in Hunter's Quay near Dunoon, for some days with a sore throat. There was a telephone with which to keep in touch. When he got there, he kissed her and was immediately aware of a strange, sweet and sickly odour. So he summoned a doctor.

The doctor took only minutes to diagnose diphtheria. This is both infectious and contagious. In a short time, the wife was in isolation in the fever hospital in Dunoon, whilst Chapman was in quarantine in his cabin in the depot ship in the Holy Loch.

Chapman did not, in fact, get the dread disease. He kicked his heels, when released from quarantine, until *Torbay* returned to the Holy Loch. There had been a change of policy. When *Torbay* returned, Chapman was reclaimed, *vice* David Verschoyle-Campbell who had replaced him as navigating officer.

Little could Chapman, and Miers, know how well this contretemps was destined in future to serve them.

4 The Clyde to Alexandria

We join the 'Iron Ring', reach Gibraltar and find acid in the battery sumps and flooding in the Asdic's oscillator

Torbay had not been able to give anything more than overnight leave since Chatham. Thus, a day or so after returning from the abortive trip to Canada, half the crew, plus the first lieutenant, engineer officer and third hand, went on five days leave. They caught the afternoon ferry with a view to the night express Glasgow to Euston. This left Miers, half a crew and Chapman as acting first lieutenant and permanent duty officer. It was 21 March 1941.

At 0100 on 22 March Miers came down to rouse his duty, and only, officer. *Torbay* was to sail at 1600, that day, for an 'Iron Ring' patrol in the Bay of Biscay. The German battle-cruisers *Scharnhorst* and *Gneisenau* were still holed up in Brest. They had been on forays into the Atlantic, where they had done immense damage to shipping. If ever it seemed that they were poised again to sally forth, all the submarines that Admiral Submarines could muster were sent to patrol positions in concentric rings round Brest. Hence came the term 'Iron Ring'. Indeed, some very old iron was mobilized for the purpose.

Miers judged that his people would be passing Carlisle heading south. It seemed that we might have them intercepted at Euston with instructions to proceed at once to Falmouth; there they might wait for us and rejoin.

However, this was ruled out on the grounds that *Torbay* must get into position as soon as possible, so that a diversion to Falmouth could not be allowed. That being so, Miers had to recruit or borrow three officers and half a crew. In the meantime, Chapman was to prepare for sea and get the depot ship staff, who had been roused, to remedy as many as possible of the outstanding defects by tea-time.

Chapman enquired whether his capacity was as fourth hand or as acting first lieutenant. The answer was 'You will be first lieutenant.' Miers and Chapman had known each other for seventy-four days. Miers managed to borrow an engineer officer who was standing by a submarine building at Greenock. He retrieved David Verschoyle-Campbell, who had done the Canada trip, and found another sub-lieutenant, Roy Foster; also he got half a crew from the depot ship spare crew. Not in all cases could the most appropriate person be found. For example, there was no spare cook, so that an able seaman was made cook. *Torbay* duly set off at tea-time and headed for the Irish Sea.

In the allotted position in the Bay of Biscay the weather was bad, sometimes appalling. It was a constant struggle to keep a periscope watch, and the pitching and rolling at night made things very uncomfortable. How *Torbay* would have fared had *Scharnhorst* and *Gneisenau* turned up is problematical. The scratch crew had never fired a torpedo, and one could hardly imagine pitting a scratch 4-inch gun's crew against battle-cruisers with, no doubt, destroyer and air escort.

There was also a problem in relation to torpedo attack, in rough weather, against the *Scharnhorst* and *Gneisenau* ('*Scharnhorst* and *Gneisenau*, weak at the knees now' sang the fore planesman; not quite the right pronunciation for *Gneisenau*, but we knew what he had in mind). The problem was that periscope depth was really only practicable with the sea and swell on *Torbay*'s beam. But would that be a suitable course for firing? Almost certainly not. Then what? It was possible, having identified the enemy, to go deep and to fire on a Sonar, or line of sound, bearing. But in those days this would be nothing like so accurate as using line of sight.

The problem remained, both haunting and intractable, to the extent that the first lieutenant had a nightmare. In this, the enemy turned up and Miers was ordered to surface and to fire a seventeen-gun salute; then the first lieutenant wound the fore hydroplane wheel, and, like a barrel organ, it played '*Deutschland Über Alles*'. Well, really, worries did lead to some muddled thoughts at night.

It was the case, however, that if the enemy had come out and had passed fairly close, the first warning would probably have been hearing hydrophone effect on the Sonar. This was because, at periscope depth by day, you hardly ever saw much beyond the top of the next wave.

It is right to mention the extent to which Miers stood in for, and nursed, his very green first lieutenant. The trial trim dive in the Clyde had shown that *Torbay* was heavy by the stern; that would mean 'bubble forward' as opposed to the desirable 'bubble aft', as explained in Chapter 2. Since the abortive Canada trip, *Torbay* had topped up with fuel, fresh water and distilled water, and the result was as described.

The most used auxiliary ballast tanks were 'A', right forward, 'O', amidships, and 'Z', right aft. There were others, but the aforementioned three were primary. To correct the unwanted bubble forward condition, the first lieutenant had pumped from 'Z' until it was empty, and still *Torbay* was heavy aft. Now, you really should always have some water, on which to veer and haul, in all three of 'A', 'O' and 'Z'.

As *Torbay* went down the Irish Sea, the first lieutenant and the chief stoker, who was one of the newcomers and thus did not know *Torbay*'s idiosyncrasies, settled down with pencil and paper to determine the reason for the condition and to decide what ballast water to shift from whence to whither. Miers had advised them to take levels of all auxiliary ballast tanks, and of fresh and distilled water tanks, and then to compare with the 'Trim Book' record of when *Torbay* had last dived; this was during the Canada trip. The Trim Book was made up at intervals, and, if this was conscientiously done, you could get

auxiliary ballast-tank readings for a variety of conditions –
for example, with torpedoes and ammunition embarked,
and without the same.

The trouble was tracked down to no. 4 fresh water tank.
It was by far the largest one, it was very close to the stern,
and it was three parts empty towards the end of the
Canada trip. In the Holy Loch it had been topped up to its
capacity of 4,000 gallons. Chapman's predecessor had
made some allowance for this, but obviously nothing like
enough. Various adjustments were made, and 500 gallons
were put into 'Z' for veer and haul. When *Torbay* next
dived, she was in the Bay of Biscay; the trim was
practically right.

When the trim problem had been sorted out, the first
lieutenant thought about the 'watch and station bill'. This
specified watch and special duties of each individual crew
member. But Miers, having interviewed each of the
newcomers, had already done it for him.

During this period in the Bay of Biscay, Miers was
dissuaded from what may be considered a pernicious
habit. When he wanted to dive, he merely ordered that the
klaxon horns be sounded twice. In the North Sea patrols,
which the first lieutenant had done, this procedure was
reserved for a genuine emergency. For a routine dive,
such as at the dawning of day, the order 'diving stations'
was passed through the boat by word of mouth; then the
engines were stopped; then the order to dive was given;
all this was in relatively slow time, with nobody rushing
about and tripping over each other.

Miers' habit, had he persisted, would have got people so
blasé at the sound of the klaxon that there would have
been a slow turn-out in a real emergency. The moral is, of
course, 'Never cry "Wolf".' Miers readily accepted the
arguments adduced.

It may be asked, 'Why iron rings of submarines, as we had
battleships and battle-cruisers?' The *Scharnhorst* and
Gneisenau could outrun these, as they had when the
battle-cruiser *Renown* tried to get at them off Narvik in
April 1940. The *Gneisenau* was considerably damaged, yet

they managed to show a clean pair of heels. Of course, this was rather absurd; the fast, well-armoured *Scharnhorst* and *Gneisenau* should have been able to see off the elderly, lightly armoured *Renown*. The latter had six 15-inch guns, whilst the enemy had between them eighteen 11-inch guns. However, the German Navy had entered the war woefully deficient as regards ships of all kinds in relation to Britain and France. We all know that there was not much wrong with the German Army and Air Force, but it takes longer to build ships than it does tanks and planes. The German Navy had counted on no war with 'England', as they still called it until 1944 or 1945.* Thus it was that the German Naval Command was obsessed with preserving what fleet they had 'in being'; and their people were encouraged to massacre the weak but not to take on anything that might be termed 'superior force'. This is a pusillanimous philosophy which leads to missed opportunity; had it been prevalent at the times in question, the British would not have gone into the attack at such battles as Cape Saint Vincent (1797), Trafalgar (1805) and the River Plate (1939). These are just three of many examples; but lest we get too cocky, remember that it was precisely a muddled order, about not engaging 'superior force', that allowed the German *Goeben* and *Breslau* to get from Algeria, past the British cruiser patrols, scot-free to Turkey; there they nudged Turkey into the war on the German side.**

Even so, back to the question, 'Why not a surface force patrolling off Brest to intercept, as in the days of such as Nelson, Collingwood and Cornwallis?' The force would have been spotted by German reconnaissance aircraft, so that the enemy could simply wait until it went away. That would not take long, because the Royal Navy then had virtually no arrangements for replenishing fuel, ammunition and stores at sea; to do that meant returning to harbour; then the stable door would be wide open. But the main and compelling reason related to air power and to

* See *Hitler and His Admirals* by Anthony Martienssen (Secker & Warburg, 1948).
** See *The Ship that Changed the World* by Dan van der Vat (Hodder & Stoughton, 1985).

U-boats. To have a reasonable chance of intercepting the fast-moving enemy, a force would have to be stationed fairly close to Brest. But then it would be subject to intensive air attack by aircraft based in France reinforced by others switched from the Low Countries and Norway; submarines – U-boats, that is – would be summoned from wherever they were. No surface force can survive continuous air attack unless it has its own air support, both to provide fighter defence and to suppress the enemy air effort at its bases. The Royal Navy had neither enough carriers nor the right sort of aircraft in them to do this; the Royal Air Force fighters could not reach the area.

However, before leaving the point, be it noted that, when *Scharnhorst* and *Gneisenau* did eventually come out, in February 1942, it was only to make a dash for home up the English Channel. In the course of this, *Gneisenau* was mined twice and took no further part in the war; *Scharnhorst* was mined once; she was repaired in time to be sunk at the battle of the North Cape at Christmas 1943. In the meantime, Royal Air Force bombers and torpedo bombers had constantly set back the efforts to prepare the ships for sea.

In the circumstances of 1941, the only Royal Navy force that could hang around off Brest was the submarines. There they were, for periods of weeks, unsupported and undetected; because the Germans had no radar-equipped aircraft to find them on the surface at night. The Germans had no means of knowing if, nor where, nor how many; the submarines would have orders not to disclose their presence by attacking targets of opportunity; and, of course, they would not give themselves away by making radio signals.

Here we pause briefly to consider what happened to some of the people *Torbay* had left behind in the Glasgow to Euston express. First Lieutenant Paul Skelton went to the submarine command course; then he was given command of a submarine that was to be delivered to Turkey; thus we saw him in Alexandria about New Year 1942. Later he was killed when the aircraft in which he was a passenger crashed.

Many of the ratings, including such important people as the electrical artificer and the gunlayer, went to the submarine *Cachalot*. *Cachalot* arrived in Alexandria some three months after *Torbay*, and her captain, Lieutenant Hugo Roland Barnwell Newton, considered himself in honour bound to offer these people 'repatriation' to *Torbay*. Miers and Chapman had reservations: our 'scratch' crew had by then settled down, and a further upheaval might be the reverse of a good idea. However, the question never arose, because the people concerned elected to stay with Newton.

As it turned out, the ex-*Torbays* made the wrong decision: *Cachalot* was rammed and sunk at night near Sicily, and her people finished up as prisoners of war in Italy. Cachalot's first lieutenant, 'Jeff' Dixon, managed to escape in the confusion after the Italian surrender; he reached the British lines near Foggia; the others were carted off to Germany.

After some long time, so it seemed, but in fact only about two weeks, we had a message; 'Remain on patrol to limit of endurance.' When Miers made this known, the cook's comment was to the effect that that was last week. However, we had to work out how we stood. There was fuel and food in abundance, even if the food was mainly bully beef and biscuits. We had our complete outfit of torpedoes and ammunition. But we were already down to some forty per cent of our fresh water; we had not been rationing it, as we had not expected the message that we had got. It seemed that fresh water was sure to be the first thing to run out, and we had no means of distilling any sensible quantity. So we took the pressure off the fresh-water tanks, which meant that taps would not run, and we issued water for drinking, cooking and washing up, in kettles. Washing was banned, except in salt water; we did have some salt-water soap, but it was nothing like the real thing. Another measure was to dilute the fresh water we did issue with distilled water from the tanks designed to top up the main batteries.

It was not long after this that we got a further message: 'Your services are urgently required in the Mediterranean. Proceed to Gibraltar. I will do my best about your gear.' This last was because, as we were expecting to return to the Clyde, we had embarked only the essentials before sailing. (Our gear was a saga destined to last more than a year, and the tale will be told when it reached completion.)

Having digested this, Miers made it generally known. Several problems attended him. We had expected to recover our old crew, or most of them. Mr Giordan, the engineer officer we had borrowed, must return to continue his supervision of an S-class submarine building at Scott's in Greenock. But what about the other officers and men? Miers asked Chapman to speak with him in the captain's cabin.

'Would you be prepared to stay as you now are?'

'Yes, but do you not think that you could find someone with more experience from the submarine depot ship at Gibraltar?'

'Had that been what I wanted, I would not have asked you.'

'Well, sir, thank you.'

We changed engineer officers at Gibraltar. Tono Kidd joined, and Mr Giordan went home. We changed the torpedo gunner's mate, since ours had shown that, though willing, he was too old to stand the rigours of a long patrol. But otherwise the scratch crew, thrown together overnight, remained. In particular, Miers would have nothing to do with the suggestion, by the captain submarines at Gibraltar, that he should ship an older and more experienced second in command. There was method in his madness. His first lieutenant was so very junior that he would probably stay for the whole commission. (In fact, he did.) A more senior person would almost certainly have been called to the submarine command course half way through. There are always dangers in breaking up what has to be a team.

There was another factor. Between early January and mid March Miers had taken unusual trouble to test and train Chapman. The latter was navigating, signals and confidential books, and correspondence officer. Nevertheless, Miers had caused him to load a salvo of torpedoes, to stand in for the signalman on the bridge, to take *Torbay* alongside the depot ship swinging to the wind at a single buoy, and to do a submerged attack, dummy, of course, *in loco* commanding officer. These tasks had been performed rather well. Miers had studied the credentials, and knew the strengths and weaknesses, in a way that would have to start all over again with a stranger. In fact, he had for some time concluded that, sooner or later, he would like Chapman to be first lieutenant. The way the cookie had crumbled, he was able to produce a *fait accompli*, sooner.

> On the strength of one link in the cable
> Dependeth the might of the chain.
> Who knows when thou mayest be tested?
> So live that thou bearest the strain.
>
> From 'The Laws of the Navy'

With the arrival of Tono Kidd was completed 'The Hard Core' of supporters who were to remain with Sir Tony for the rest of the commission. They were Kidd, Campbell and Chapman. The remaining complement billet was filled, from time to time, by no fewer than four other officers. Often we had an extra 'fifth hand', or a midshipman, embarked for training and experience; a useful job they did, but they were not in complement.

Sometimes there may have been difficulties, sometimes disagreements; but the fact is that the 'other officer' came and went at intervals. That is, until Tony Melville-Ross arrived. He stayed; moreover, he became first lieutenant for *Torbay*'s second commission in the Mediterranean.

For entering harbour at Gibraltar, Chapman was reluctant to risk one of the suits with two stripes; he suggested that he might go in wearing a relatively old one still with only one stripe. Miers was enthusiastic: 'Oh yes, I will go in with three sub-lieutenants; that will make them think.'

The spare submarine commanding officer at Gibraltar was one Richard Favell; it was his business to explain to the newly arrived submarine such things as mess-deck and cabin accommodation, and any special requirements to match depot ship routine. Favell had last seen Chapman, in December 1940 in the Clyde, as the relatively humble sub-lieutenant navigator of *H 34*. Moreover, he had observed him slipping ashore with, amongst other things, a sword. A sword is not the sort of thing that a young officer on leave normally needs unless a wedding is involved; thus Favell had been the first to unlock the secret.

Looking down, Favell could see nothing that looked like a first lieutenant; this was after Miers had gone inboard.

Favell called, 'Is your first lieutenant there?'

Chapman replied, 'I will have him speak with you directly, sir.'

Then Chapman went down the conning-tower hatch, through the boat, up the fore hatch and up the accommodation ladder to HMS *Maidstone*'s well deck; then, with a smart salute, 'I understand that you want the first lieutenant, sir.'

Favell's first reaction was to offer hearty congratulations; he added, 'You are a one for springing surprises.'

In the evening of our arrival at Gibraltar, Petty Officer Rayner, in charge of batteries and main motors, sought out Chapman in the depot ship.

His news was sombre. There was a minor earth on the batteries, and he had found traces of acid in all three battery sumps. The batteries were of the lead acid type, the acid being hydrochloric. If these symptoms meant what they might mean, it was serious indeed. Rayner's and Chapman's knowledge indicated that some of the 336 battery cells were cracked and leaking. For this the remedy was to find out which ones, hoist them out and replace them. This could take a week or more, with the whole living-compartments in an uproar, and amongst other things a crane would be needed.

They decided that they must alert Miers. Here his experience was decisive. He listened to the news and to the diagnosis. Then he pointed out that, were the diagnosis correct, the batteries should have shown signs of fading performance. But they had not so shown. He reminded us that the batteries had been topped up with distilled water a few days before we sailed from the Holy Loch. The very heavy rolling in the Bay of Biscay had caused a small amount of dilute acid to slop over and gradually to seep down to the sumps. If the minor earth remained much the same, he was right. If it developed to a full earth, we were right. It did not develop, and we had a minor and unimportant earth on the batteries for the rest of the commission.

The cracked container drama was against a strange background. When *Torbay* reached Gibraltar, on 13 April, we were astonished to learn that we were to sail, for patrol and Alexandria, after a twenty-four-hour stop-over. We had been at sea, in most uncomfortable conditions, for twenty-two days. The powers-that-were expected *Torbay* to go straight on for a further three-week patrol, including passage through the hot spot of the Sicilian Narrows. All our main armament of sixteen torpedoes needed to be serviced, a job of about a week. The tired scratch crew had done no working-up exercises together. *Torbay* duly set off eastwards on 14 April.

If there were to be a *Guinness Book of Bad Judgements*, no doubt this decision, for which the captain, commander and staff officer submarines must be held responsible, should have a place. All three are now dead, so there let us leave it.

Captain 'Sammy' Raw, at Alexandria, did not leave it. As soon as he saw what had happened, from signals (not that *Torbay* had made any), he invited Gibraltar to recall us for at least a week's rest. So we had time to service our torpedoes. *Torbay* sailed for the second time, for patrol and Alexandria, on 22 April.

This time we had with us a senior lieutenant-commander from the United States Navy. He was a submariner; he took his turn at periscope and surface watch. Yet it was nearly eight months before the United States was at war. My generation will never forget such demonstrations of helpful interest, of which this was just one tiny example. The American's name was Frank T. Watkins, and he was later to be the United States Comsublant (Commander Submarines Atlantic).

The three-week trip was relatively uneventful. An unescorted merchant vessel was sighted close west of Sardinia, and Miers sought to attack her with three torpedoes, spread to allow for errors in course and speed estimations. To his chagrin, she sailed serenely on. The gun option was not on, because there was a patrolling aircraft in sight.

Later the torpedo gunner's mate (TGM) came to offer profuse apology. Owing to errors in drill, only one torpedo, not three, had been fired. Well, as said before, the scratch crew had never fired a torpedo. Moreover, the TGM had joined us only the day before we had left Gibraltar for the second time.

Five days out from Gibraltar, the Asdic went out of action. There was no insulation on the oscillator, so it seemed that it must have flooded; but how? The oscillator was in a cage at the front end of the keel, say about fourteen feet under water; the only way to get it out for inspection was to raise it, take off the hatch cover in the torpedo stowage compartment and lift it out. But this would mean that the largest compartment in the boat would be open to flooding while the hatch cover was off. A submarine can not remain afloat with its torpedo stowage compartment flooded.

Most people would have given it up as a bad job, until return to harbour; but not Miers. The torpedo stowage compartment was shut off from the tube space forward of it. Tono Kidd, the engineer, with helpers, was put into the torpedo stowage compartment. Then the door to the crew space was shut, and the first lieutenant put in a pressure of some fifteen pounds per square inch. This was about double the external sea pressure, and so inhibited flooding. The pressure had to be topped up as the air bubbled out of the keel; so the first lieutenant's prayer was that the low-pressure air blowers would not blow their fuses. But, in case they did, he had connected the high-pressure air (3,000 pounds per square inch) salvage blow. When the pressure was enough a signal to Tono gave him the go-ahead. There was no telephone in the torpedo stowage compartment, so signals each way had to be hammer blows on the bulkhead.

They got the oscillator up, replaced the hatch cover, signalled completion and were let out. During this operation, which was carried out on the surface at night in enemy waters, *Torbay* could not dive. Consequently there was another signal to Tono which meant, 'Stop everything and put back the hatch cover.' The oscillator was dried out for a week and then replaced by the same methods as it had been brought out. It managed adequate reception, but it would not transmit. But this latter was a rare requirement; it was reception that really mattered, to give us warning of the approach of enemy surface craft.

As regards the Sicilian Narrows, Miers decided that the bold course was the safest. Instead of creeping through dived by day at about 3 knots, *Torbay* charged through at 14 knots on the surface by night on 5/6 May.

Still making eastwards, *Torbay* did a close periscope reconnaissance of Navarin harbour in the Peloponnese. But there was nothing there worth having; so slowly on, aiming to arrive Alexandria on 13 May.

In the night preceding *Torbay*'s approach to Alexandria, Chapman, as officer of the watch on the surface, saw a group of ships to the north-east. He increased speed, altered course towards an attacking position and was joined on the bridge by Miers; the latter made preparations to attack with torpedoes.

It was bright moonlight. Soon, the chunky, unmistakable silhouettes of *Queen Elizabeth*-class battleships, nothing like the sleek lines of Italian battleships, showed that the force was ours. But we did not know that they were out, nor did they expect to meet us. This was a lapse of staff work, of which there were all too many. One shudders to think what might have happened on a darker night. *Torbay* was in a prime firing position and could have sunk two of our own battleships.

Torbay had reached the fringe of the inner destroyer

screen when the position was clear beyond any doubt. She turned away and fired a recognition signal in the form of a pyrotechnic grenade. This should have indicated to all that we were friendly. However, the signal drew no such response as 'Hullo, how are you?' What *Torbay* got was a burst of Oerlikon gunfire from the nearest destroyer, which was by then very near.

Miers had a very fine voice when he chose to use it. He stood up on a step at the side of the bridge and tried another form of recognition. He roared at the destroyer, 'Don't be a cunt!' The firing ceased. Probably this was because the commanding officer had recognized the import of *Torbay*'s pyrotechnic and had restrained his trigger-happy gunlayer. Even so, the theory that it was Miers' stentorian voice which had stopped the rot did no harm to his image in the eyes of *Torbay*'s people.

Torbay had inflicted no damage on the enemy. She had, however, 'shaken down' and had carried out a complex domestic operation, which few would have even considered. She had avoided three hostile air patrols and three patrol vessels.

'Sammy' Raw commented, '*Torbay* can not be considered a fully efficient unit. But I have confidence that, under Lieutenant-Commander Miers, she will be.'

His first sentence was all too true; we were grateful for his second.

Whatever had happened before, you started the count again from one when you were assigned to the Mediterranean. So let us call the Clyde to Alexandria the 'first patrol' and then move on to the second.

5 Second Patrol – The Aegean

In which Torbay *lurks outside the Dardanelles, claiming seven victims, and survives her 'baptism of fire'*

This patrol was from 28 May to 16 June 1941.

The position was difficult. The defenders of Crete under the New Zealander General Freyberg had been overwhelmed and were being evacuated from the south of the island. There is nothing there that could be called a harbour (these are all on the north coast), but the Germans were already there. The final evacuation was on 3 June, but it left behind some 5,000 Commonwealth troops. They had permission to surrender, but not all did; they holed up in villages, mountains and monasteries, and several hundred were later rescued by various means, including *Torbay*'s fourth patrol.

The surface ships of the Mediterranean Fleet suffered heavily in the Battle of Crete and in the evacuation. Three cruisers and six destroyers were sunk, including Mountbatten's *Kelly*. Two battleships and the only aircraft-carrier, the *Formidable*, had to be sent for major repair to Durban or the United States. Very few other ships were undamaged, and the personnel were almost exhausted.

On the other side of the coin, the Germans got Crete, but at the cost of so debilitating their airborne forces that these, as such, took no further part in major operations. There were more strategically important objectives where they might have been used – for example, to capture Malta or Syria.

The Germans had to maintain their forces in Crete, and to stock and develop airfields from whence to challenge British control of the Eastern Mediterranean. The bulk of the available shipping was being used on the North Africa run, so that extensive use was made, even during the battle, of local coasters, schooners and caiques. These were not torpedo targets but were vulnerable to a submarine's gun and/or demolition charges.

There was another sort of traffic in the Aegean. Oil was an Axis weak point, and in particular the Italian Navy was constrained by shortage of fuel. The Vichy French, no longer able to trade with the rest of the world, had plenty of laid-up tankers. Stalin was still cynically supplying the Axis, though he was within a few weeks of being attacked and almost overwhelmed on 22 June 1941.

The damage to the Mediterranean Fleet, and even more so the impossibility of giving any sort of air support from North Africa, meant that the only force capable of taking the offensive in the Aegean was the First Submarine Flotilla. But not much effort could be spared from the North Africa run. Thus *Torbay* had the Aegean all to herself except for Germans, Italians, Greeks and Turks.

The problem of providing air support in the Aegean was to continue for a long time. It led to the loss of Kos, Leros and Samos in October 1943. These islands had been occupied, at about battalion strength, by troops carried thither by sea; but the unexpectedly violent German reaction with air forces and paratroops was such that the islands were recaptured. Most of the Allied troops were forced to surrender, and many ships were lost or damaged.

The only ships which could safely operate in such conditions were submarines. As has been said of them, in another context, 'Their particular advantage over other ships is the ability to operate unsupported, and often undetected, in areas where the enemy exercises maritime control.'

Tony Miers always had a plan. He made an intense study of

all the information about the area to which he had been assigned, and of enemy habits there. It resulted that he was often in the right place at the right time. Equally, his patrol reports were a mine of information and recommendations for those who were to follow after. His general plan was to make a nuisance of himself in as many places as possible, so as to cause the enemy to suspect that there were a lot more submarines about than was the case. They would then hesitate to sail important units without adequate escort. In particular he intended to include in his wanderings a position just outside Turkish territorial waters, at the entrance to the Dardanelles. First Flotilla opinion was that such a position was 'untenable' because of the current and the water (layers) conditions. Said Miers to the first lieutenant, 'We will change that. We will say that *Torbay* "tenned" it.'

A look at an atlas shows the huge rivers flowing into the Black Sea. The water has to go somewhere, else there would be a Noah-type flood of the littoral lands. So it roars through the Bosphorus to the Sea of Marmara and then at a slightly slower pace through the Dardanelles to the Mediterranean. The Mediterranean is relatively warm and loses a lot by evaporation. For the same reason, the Mediterranean is also fed, for three parts round the clock, by the Atlantic.

On 1 June *Torbay* engaged a caique flying the swastika in the Doro Channel – that is, between the isles of Andros and Euboea. After five rounds from the 4-inch gun, the caique disappeared in a violent explosion; clearly her cargo included explosives. On 3 June a caique loaded with oil drums was sunk near Mitylene, off the Turkish coast south of the Dardanelles. Then *Torbay* went on to the 'untenable' position off the Dardanelles entrance.

Well, the swirling currents were not fully described in any publication. *Torbay* found out which way she was going, when dived at 2 knots, by taking frequent navigational fixes. More often than not, we were going sideways. This put an element of extra strain on the officer of the watch, who had to fix about every fifteen minutes. The layer conditions were such that, at about fifty feet, you hit a 'feather bed' and had to take in five tons of water to get through it. There was a five-point difference in specific gravity of the water as between the surface and eighty feet depth. Flooding five tons in was quick enough* but, when you wanted to come back to periscope depth, it took ten minutes to pump it out. This meant that you would not surrender the initiative by going deep unless you really had to.

As may be imagined, there was a lot of neutral, Turkish traffic going in and out of the Dardanelles, and obviously it was taboo to attack such. Even so, one had to get reasonably close in order to identify; this meant a certain amount of relatively high submerged speed – say, 6 knots. You did not use such speeds at periscope depth of thirty-two feet; the periscope, if used, would be vibrating and would show a long feather of wash, and the thrashing propellers would make a give-away disturbance on the surface. *Torbay* would normally go to eighty feet for bursts of speed.

On arrival off the Dardanelles, Miers who had been up most of the night, had breakfast and retired for some well-earned sleep. Meanwhile the first lieutenant checked out the water conditions and found the layer already described. When Miers was soon called, because of the approach of an unidentified vessel, there had been no opportunity to explain to him the unusual conditions.

Miers wanted a burst of speed to get closer, so he ordered eighty feet. The first lieutenant countermanded to sixty feet and began to flood instead of the normal pumping to adjust for going deep. Miers was taken aback and enquired, 'What the hell do you think you are doing?' The first lieutenant had his eyes glued to the depth gauge, monitoring *Torbay*'s reactions, and was in no mood for discussion, so, 'I will explain later. Please leave this to me'; he feared that if he took *Torbay* down to eighty feet he would never get her up in time for Miers' purpose. There was a notable omission of the customary 'sir'. This, as much as anything, made Miers realize that there was

* But see Technical Appendix, p.171.

something of which he did not wot, and he held his peace.
Even so, he took early opportunity to repay the first
lieutenant in kind.

The *Alberta* was a Vichy French tanker. With a consort she
had sailed from the Marseilles area, with a mission to load
crude oil in the Black Sea and deliver to Italy. The consort
was sunk, by a submarine from Malta, in the vicinity of
Sicily, so *Alberta* went on alone towards the Dardanelles;
there *Torbay* was lurking on 6 June. *Alberta* was not
escorted.

Torbay's navigational difficulties have been described,
and *Alberta* began to be affected by the same currents. The
pair did an awkward *pas de deux* until a radical alteration of
course by *Alberta* put *Torbay* almost behind her. Miers
moved directly behind her and on the same course. From
this position he fired one torpedo on what is known as a
180-degree track – or, in layman's language, 'straight up
the kilt'. The chances of a hit, from this sort of situation,
were rated low. However, thanks to Miers' judgement and
to the accuracy of the torpedo, hit it did at 1415.

The *Alberta* was completely disabled, no rudder, no
propellers, but very far from being sunk. She did the only
thing possible: she anchored, and *Torbay* observed this.
Miers considered: there was nothing to stop her from
being towed in and repaired, thereafter to continue to do
the enemy's bidding, unless *Torbay* intervened further. So
he manoeuvred and struck *Alberta* with a second torpedo
at 1545. Still she showed no signs of sinking.

After *Alberta* had been struck for the second time, David
Campbell asked for the periscope to take a fix. We had not
had one for a long time, but he knew better than to ask for
the periscope when Miers was engaging the enemy.
Whilst doing his fix, David also took a range and bearing
of the anchored *Alberta*. Soon he announced that *Alberta*
was in Turkish territorial waters and must have been so
when first hit. In this case, technically, she should have
been immune from attack.

'Well then,' said Miers, 'she must have had bad luck.
She must have hit a mine.'

The first lieutenant ventured, 'What sort of a mine would watch in this depth and in this current?'

That was Miers' opportunity. He replied, 'Nobody asked you to speak. Please leave this to me.'

Of course, the concept was absurd. Turkey was neutral and remained so; neither side would wish to give her offence by scattering mines inside, or just outside, her territorial waters leading to her main access to the Mediterranean and Black Seas. When Turkey was a belligerent, in World War I, there had been extensive mining of the area by both sides, even as far away as the island of Imbros, fifteen miles to the north-east; it was here that the German *Goeben* and *Breslau* came to grief in 1918. But never had the *Alberta*'s position been mined, because both depth and current made those waters unsuitable.

When the first lieutenant said 'Watch', that is the technical term for a mine keeping its correct depth below the surface; no known mine would have. Anyway, it gave all concerned a good laugh.

That night, as *Alberta* was riding to her cable in the strong current, *Torbay* came alongside; she was ready with Lewis guns to fire if fired upon, but the ship was deserted; all the crew had been taken ashore. Boarding-parties were led by Kidd, the engineer, who investigated the possibilities of scuttling *Alberta*, and Campbell, who was after charts, log books and confidential publications.

Kidd had no luck. The *Alberta* was without power, and such things as valve chests were well below water in the partially flooded engine-room. Campbell had more luck: he found charts and log books which told us what she had been doing and which way she had come. For instance, she had come through the Corinth Canal, which our Intelligence rated as having been blocked by bombing raids.

Miers had hoped to scuttle *Alberta* where she was. This was not an available option, but at least he could set her adrift. Off went the torpedo gunner's mate. He had 1¼ pound demolition charges of TNT and lengths of delay-action Bickford's fuse. He made an arrangement round *Alberta's* rather massive cable and lit the fuse when ordered. Pyrotechnic flares were then set off in various places in the hope of burning *Alberta*; the petty officer was recovered, and *Torbay* backed off. In due course the charges cut the cable, and *Alberta* drifted south-westwards in the current.

These demolition charges were standard Royal Navy equipment; we had no such sophisticated stuff as plastic explosive; the charges were not unlike a litre can of beer to look at, but they were somewhat more lethal. They were ideal for blowing holes in the bottom of small craft, so as to conserve ammunition for the 4-inch gun. Such ammunition tended at times to be in short supply, as will be seen.

The whole time *Torbay* was alongside *Alberta*, she was regularly bathed in the beam of a searchlight which swept, intermittently, from Cape Helles. But this searchlight was a routine measure, and who is going to notice a relatively small submarine alongside the bulk of what would then be called a medium-sized tanker in Turkish territorial waters?

Next day, 8 June, *Alberta* was seen to be aground on Rabbit Island, south of the Dardanelles. That seemed good enough, but on the 9th she was seen under way in tow of the Turkish tug *Tirhan*. Miers fired one more torpedo, but *Tirhan* saw the large splash of discharge as the torpedo left the tube, slipped the tow and scuttled back into the Dardanelles, leaving *Alberta* adrift.

The splash of discharge, which Miers had observed through the periscope, should not have been. The torpedoes were fired with a blast of high-pressure air, and things called impulse cut-off valves were supposed to operate in such a way that there was no splash. On our return to harbour, the experts found that at some time *Torbay's* valves had been wrongly set. This might not have mattered much in the Bay of Biscay, but in the relatively calm waters of the Mediterranean it was a terrible give-away.

Shortly afterwards, an Italian destroyer came to sniff around, but she did not find *Torbay*. Shortly before 0300 on the 10th, *Torbay* sought out the drifting *Alberta*, found her and put forty 4-inch shells into her waterline. Still she would not sink; she must have had empty cargo tanks, on her centre line, which would keep a hulk afloat. However, she became a total loss.

Still on 10 June but in the forenoon, and still off the Dardanelles, a convoy of six ships escorted by two destroyers was seen approaching from the south. Miers intended to fire at the leading ship. However, just before the sights came on, he found that he was only about fifty yards on the bow of one of the destroyers. The latter would have been able to pinpoint our position from the splash of discharge. He therefore held fire and shifted target to the second ship. Soon after firing three torpedoes, *Torbay* went deep to the tune of two very loud and seemingly close explosions. The first lieutenant's thought was, 'My word! They are quick off the mark with counter-attack!' That was inexperience; they were unlikely to be so quick. Moreover, the sharp 'biff' noise was unlike the duller sound of the depth-charges we had not so far heard.

The destroyers, having reached the limit of Turkish territorial waters, in which they were not supposed to go, were dashing up and down and across and across. This was another of the disadvantages of *Torbay*'s chosen position. However, as we found out later on return to Alexandria, one of the destroyers had got in the way and had been hit by two torpedoes. That was the end of her; one torpedo would have been enough. The convoy was not hit.

The remaining destroyer counter-attacked and succeeded in landing one fairly close pattern of depth-charges. This was *Torbay*'s 'baptism of fire', and Miers was pleased to be able to report that his crew remained perfectly 'steady'. There was little damage apart from light bulbs; *Torbay* was soundly and strongly constructed.

'Steady,' said Miers. Chapman would have said 'Rock solid', even though that may be termed flamboyant. There were cases, in submarines, of people going a bit berserk when under heavy attack; this forms the basis of scenes in many a novel, but it was astonishingly rare in real life. In

Torbay's case, when under attack, Miers and Chapman would be in the control room; so would the coxswain and the second coxswain, both manning hydroplanes; so would the 'outside ERA' (the engine-room artificer responsible for machinery outside the engine-room) and the chief stoker, the first lieutenant's right-hand man in respect of auxiliary ballast tanks. Thus there was quite a concentration of talent in the control room, and these could not monitor what was going on in the fore and after parts of the submarine.

Even so, had there been any sign of faltering or panic, the senior ratings in the ends of the boat would have told the first lieutenant at the first opportunity; no such report ever came his way; *Torbay*'s people were not that sort of people. In harbour one day the first lieutenant overheard a stoker say, 'Oh yes, Miers will get us into trouble, and he will get us out of it.' Chapman believes that they would have gone on thinking that way until they found themselves dead or swimming.

The *Giuseppina Ghiradi* was an Italian tanker which had loaded crude in the Black Sea. Alexandria had warned *Torbay* to expect her to leave the Dardanelles about 10 June. Out she duly came on the appointed day and was torpedoed at 1300. Being fully loaded, unlike the empty *Alberta*, she was not at all reluctant to sink. The remaining destroyer in the area was low on charges, and the counter-attack was mild. The destroyer had been joined by two motor anti-submarine boats (MASB), otherwise Miers would have been tempted to try to attack her.

Having stirred up the Dardanelles and being towards the end of the patrol, *Torbay* headed south for the Doro Channel. On the way, at 0030 on the 11th, a Greek caique carrying military stores was encountered. The crew were allowed to leave and the craft was destroyed by repeated ramming, not too hard lest we damage our bow in general and the external torpedo tubes in particular.

On the 12th, in the Doro Channel, a large Italian schooner was sighted. She carried troops, ammunition and stores; she was sunk by gunfire.

Two tankers, one destroyer, one schooner and three caiques had been written off. Eight air and five surface patrols had been met. Twenty-one depth-charges had been experienced. *Torbay* had 'blooded' both torpedoes and gun.

Captain Sammy Raw signalled to *Torbay*: 'I knew from the enemy's distress signals that you had been busy with torpedoes; now I learn that gun and ram have also been active. Take off the "L" plates.'

The captain's covering letter to the Commander-in-Chief included: 'A brilliantly conducted patrol; *Torbay* has reached a very high standard.'

The Commander-in-Chief commented: 'It is to their great credit that *Torbay* has reached such a high standard so early.'

The Flotilla wag put things somewhat differently: '*Torbay* has grown from puberty to adultery; it really is disgusting, taking advantage of an unsuspecting French lady.'

2nd and 3rd Patrols 1941

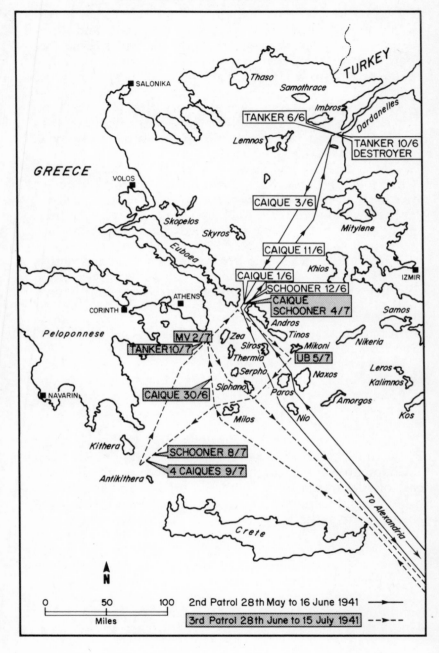

6 Third Patrol – The Aegean

We bag a U-boat, engage in 'The Battle of the Caiques' and give no quarter

This patrol was from 28 June to 15 July. The account was opened by the sinking of a caique off Phalonnera, north-west of the isle of Milos, on 30 June.

It was during the rest period between *Torbay*'s second and third patrols that Hitler launched his attack on the Soviet Union on 22 June 1941.

There was some fluttering in the domestic dovecotes by the 'Nervous Nellies'; many of the European ladies in Egypt had contemplated Beirut, Baghdad or Tehran as safe haven, and with resident diplomatic staff, in the event that Rommel got too close to Egypt. But now the nervous imagined Hitler storming through the Caucasus into Persia (Iran) and thence to Iraq, Syria and Lebanon.

Chapman was walking past the beach huts at Sidi Bish, east of Alexandria town, with the urbane and imperturbable Consul-General Clifford Heathcote-Smith, when an anxious lady asked for advice as to whither she might go. 'I suggest that you should not think about that, madam; what you should be thinking is that we have a lot more people on our side than we had the day before yesterday.'

Yes, there were some 'Nervous Nellies', but there were others quite different. The expatriates looked after the Mediterranean Fleet very well, as indeed Chapman had experienced in Singapore, the Dutch East Indies and

China. In Egypt he remembers happy times as the house guest of the families Job and Seidl, and with Teddy and Eudora Gleave in Cairo. The Seidls were Swiss, but that was appropriate in that Chapman was born in Switzerland.

Folbots and folboteers came from Captain Roger Courtney's Special Boat Section based with the First Submarine Flotilla at Alexandria.* Roger is long since dead; 'Jumbo', his younger brother, joined the SBS in due course, but some time after the period under review.

The SBS were predominantly soldiers, but there were some Royal Marines; they were people who liked 'messing about in boats'. Later they used more sophisticated craft, but in *Torbay*'s day their basic equipment was a folbot; it was before the days of fibre glass, so that a folbot was a wooden frame canoe, with a canvas skin not unlike an Eskimo kayak. It could carry the driver and a passenger and some stores. Its motive power was by a long double-bladed paddle, which was operated alternately each side of the craft by rhythmic movement of arms and shoulders; it made no noise and thus was *par excellence* a stealth weapon.

The possession of a folbot, with a trained operator, added an extra dimension to a submarine's repertoire. The submarine had no boats of its own, so that the addition of the folbot meant that you could reconnoitre harbours and beaches, land agents and generally establish communication with the shore. Originally the folbots were not purpose-built to go in submarines; they were peace-time pleasure boats co-opted for war. When fully rigged, they would not go through the submarine's forward, or torpedo, hatch. The centre frame had to be put in diagonally, then it had to be secured in its proper position athwartships on the casing in the dark. *Torbay* introduced a small modification to make the latter task more easy.

On this patrol *Torbay* had two folboteers, Corporals George Bremner and Jim Sherwood. As it turned out, they had no opportunity to exercise the folbot role (though

* See 'Jumbo' Courtney's *SBS in World War II* (Hale, 1983).

Bremner was crucial on the next patrol); but they took a full part in other ways, as look-outs and planesman and in domestic chores and, more importantly, manning the bridge Lewis guns during surface action. At this stage, bren-guns, which were far more reliable, had not yet been issued to Alexandria submarines. The Lewis guns were temperamental pests, constantly subject to jams, 'double feed first phase' and all that, as the writer remembers from his midshipman's musketry course at Stonecutters Island off Kowloon, which is opposite Hong Kong. A soldier was better trained to deal with malfunction than was a sailor.

Also, one remembers George Bremner, squatting on his haunches on *Torbay's* saddle tanks, covering with his tommy-gun *Torbay's* party boarding caiques.

Miers was quick to see the extra opportunities presented by folboteers, and from the third patrol onward *Torbay* usually had one or more. A number of important operations would have been impossible without them.

On 2 July two merchant vessels escorted by two destroyers were sighted in the Zea Channel – that is, south of the Doro Channel and between the isle of Keos and the Greek mainland. The sea was still glassy calm. The previous day we had noted that we could see the details of our own hull through the periscope. Three torpedoes were fired at each merchant ship. The leading ship, which proved to be the *Città di Tripoli*, was struck and sunk at 0722. The second ship, alerted by the fate of her consort, managed to alter course to avoid her share. The counter-attack, when eighteen depth-charges were dropped, was ineffective.

Here one may note that, in the summer in the Eastern Mediterranean, the layer conditions made it relatively easy for a submarine to evade the then anti-submarine techniques, but in winter and spring, when there were fewer layers, conditions were far more favourable to anti-submarine craft.

We were to learn, later, from Lieutenant Raymond, United States Navy, who was with us during *Torbay's* eleventh patrol, that if we had had American torpedo-angling equipment, the ship behind *Città di Tripoli* might not have got away. The two ships were fairly far apart. Having fired upon the first, Miers waited for the second to cross his sights. Of course, it would have been possible to alter course, and even to fire whilst still 'On the swing', but this is more error-prone than a more deliberate attack.

Even so, the British method meant that two salvoes, each of three torpedoes, arrived some minutes apart; thus the second ship was alerted by the fate of the first. With the American system, the second salvo would have been angled and would have left *Torbay* immediately after the first. In that case, the second ship would have had only seconds of warning, and that would not have been enough.

The wind arose that night, and on 3 July the sea was quite rough. Miers contemplated trying to torpedo an anti-submarine trawler. But, in view of the sea state, it was doubtful if the torpedoes would run correctly at the necessarily fairly shallow depth setting. The attempt was abandoned.

The following day a caique and a schooner, both flying the swastika, were sighted south-east of Doro Island. They were troop-carrying. The troops were not allowed to escape: everything and everybody were destroyed by one sort of gunfire or another. Much the same was to happen on 9 July, so comment will be deferred until the later incident.

Torbay had moved eastwards and was off the isle of Mykoni on the evening of 5 July. At 1946 the Italian U-boat *Jantina* was sighted on the surface at a range of about four miles. Admittedly Italian U-boats then had exaggeratedly large and high conning towers; you would hardly have seen a German U-boat at four miles through a periscope. Even so, the early sighting showed that there was nothing wrong with the look-out being kept by the officer of the watch, Roy Foster. Miers was able to carry out an unhurried attack.

Jantina was westbound, close to the southern shore of Mykoni. At 2016 six torpedoes were fired at a range of about 1,500 yards; two or possibly three hit; there was a huge explosion which broke *Torbay*'s own navigation lights. Soon an aircraft appeared, but by then he had no idea where we were. What *Jantina* was doing off Mykoni is hard to imagine; there was nothing British around except *Torbay*.

It sounds rather easy but, in fact, attacking U-boats was not. Quite apart from spotting one in the first place, as Foster had, there is not a lot to see. Unlike a surface ship, a surfaced submarine is like an iceberg, mostly under water; thus it is that, until she is very close, you may never see her bow, casing and stern; you may see only the oval-cum-cylindrical-shaped conning tower. To judge from that which way she is going and how fast is a job for an expert. But there are helps: successive observations of enemy bearing and range should provide, when plotted, an estimate of both course and speed, so that the navigating officer may come up with a report such as, 'Plot suggests 250 degrees, 13 knots'; the Sonar operator will count engine revolutions per minute, which is another speed indication; in the case of the *Jantina*, close to Mykoni, her position on the chart gave an indication of course; for example, she would hardly be steering north to run on the rocks.

When the event was over, and *Torbay*'s people fell out from 'diving stations', the first lieutenant had the watch. To him came David Campbell, who traced the outline of a Distinguished Service Cross on Chapman's left breast. 'You think so?' 'Together with what we have already done, I know so.' And, in fact, it was so; but the first lieutenant's thoughts had been quite different; they had been: 'Last October an Italian submarine did for my brother Patrick, as first lieutenant of the submarine *Rainbow*, in the Golfo di Taranto; now it is one-all.'

Firing at the *Jantina* was the first occasion on which *Torbay* had fired six torpedoes in rapid succession – say, eight seconds between each torpedo. When a submarine fired a torpedo, she lost two tons in weight and was that much the lighter, particularly by the bow. A system known as 'automatic inboard venting' (AIV) admitted water to the torpedo tube, and to an AIV tank because the torpedo was heavier than a tube full of water. But the system took a little time to complete its work. Thus a submarine, firing torpedoes rapidly, would get progressively lighter for a temporary period.

The standard remedy, to prevent the submarine's leaping to the surface, was to flood 'Q' tank, after the second torpedo left, and to blow it when AIV had settled down. Chapman had watched this during torpedo-discharge trials at Arrochar in Loch Long. Inevitably, flooding 'Q' took the submarine down to forty feet or more, so that the periscope was dipped and the captain could not see at what might be an important moment.

Torbay never used 'Q' tank to compensate for torpedo fire. She started with 'bubble aft', as explained in Chapter 2, and the planesman held her down. Admittedly, *Torbay* might rise from thirty-two to twenty-seven feet; but at least the captain could see. Bubble aft was not a foregone conclusion. It should be so at watch diving routine, but, when you order 'diving stations', which is submarine for 'action stations', a whole lot of men who normally live and sleep forward of amidships go to the centre or further aft. This tends to put the bubble forward, so that the first lieutenant's first task at diving stations was to transfer ballast water to restore bubble aft. And this had to be done at once; we knew, from the noise trials in Loch Long, that our ballast pumps were noisy. Thus, in the late stages of an attack, when the enemy were close, ballast pumps were taboo, lest the enemy's escort be by them alerted.

Torbay moved westwards to the Kithera Channel to the north-west of Crete. On 8 July a swastika-flying schooner was destroyed. This action, from 1120 to 1140, was interrupted by the appearance of an aircraft. The latter did not see what was happening and flew away; so *Torbay*, having dived, came up again to finish the job.

'The Battle of the Caiques' was what we called the happenings between 0220 and 0536 on 9 July. There were four caiques and one schooner between the isles of Kithera and Antikithera; they were coming from Crete towards Cape Malea in the Peloponnese, but when *Torbay* appeared, they scattered and made to escape towards Antikithera. The troops on board were probably German 11th Air Corps who had conquered Crete and had now been relieved by garrison troops.

When the action was completed, four of the craft, and all that therein was, had been destroyed. The fifth got away. *Torbay* was already low in 4-inch ammunition, so this was used sparingly. The range was closed until Lewis guns could come into play, and the craft would sometimes be boarded and sunk by demolition charges.

In one case a caique hailed us: 'Captain is Greek; we surrender.' But it did not sound like a Greek voice. When we got alongside, Corporal Bremner, our embarked soldier folboteer, saw an individual about to throw a grenade. Bremner shot him. Then Campbell, on the casing ready to board, saw one pointing a rifle at him from behind the wheelhouse. Campbell shot him, and we shot the lot. Fanatical Nazis make treacherous companions. When daylight came, there were aircraft searching all over the place, so some of the action must have been observed from shore, which was fairly close; *Torbay* sighted nine aircraft during the day.

It may be thought that *Torbay*'s actions on 4 and 9 July were unduly harsh. There was no complaint from Sir Andrew Cunningham, nor from Captain Raw, but some eyebrows were raised in London, by flag officer submarines and within the Admiralty. It finished with the ruling by the vice-chief of naval staff: 'The man on the spot must decide what is necessary at the time.'

London could not have known the rather horrid circumstances of the Battle of Crete as well as did *Torbay*. The German 11th Air Corps were fanatical ex-Hitler Jugend. Their Stuka element, so long as they had fuel remaining, stooged around machine-gunning survivors in the water. They gave no quarter, and *Torbay* was like-minded in respect of them. They would have fared no better had they been blasted out of the water by the guns of cruisers and destroyers, as happened during the battle. As has been said, the Mediterranean surface forces were no longer in a position to operate anywhere near Crete.

Furthermore, as indicated in Chapter 5, any German development of their new bases in Crete and the Aegean islands was bad for British interests. Traffic to or from was to be interdicted, and only the submarines were in a position to do it. In particular, Germans getting to Crete was bad news; even if they had arrived wearing birthday suits, such was the plenty of arms, ammunition and other kit, from corpses of both sides, that they could almost at once have been incorporated into a unit. It was also the case that there were still a lot of Commonwealth troops on the run in Crete, as told in Chapters 5 and 7.

The Germans had had setbacks at sea – *Graf Spee, Altmark*, Narvik, where they lost about half their destroyer force – and in the air, in the Battle of Britain. On the other hand their land campaigns had been almost victory parades: Poland, Norway, Denmark, the Netherlands, Belgium, France, Yugoslavia, Greece. They did not like what happened in Crete, where they came up against mainly Anzac bone. In their own words, they suffered exceptionally bloody losses.

The struggle for Crete led to an escalation of violence, by both sides, as moods and tempers grew ever uglier. When, during the battle, our surface forces were still operating, at night, north of Crete, they would sometimes come across caique convoys such as did *Torbay*. I never heard of a single prisoner being taken.

Strombo was a loaded tanker which was sunk at 1500 on 10 July in the Zea Channel. *Torbay* used her four remaining torpedoes; six had been fired at the *Città di Tripoli* and her consort, and six at the *Jantina*, so four it had to be. *Strombo* had a destroyer with her; she dropped twenty-five depth-charges. An hour after the end of *Strombo*, three destroyers and an aircraft searched. The destroyers dropped thirty-eight depth-charges, which were duly recorded on the chief stoker's blackboard.

The destroyers did not get close enough to detect, or to do any damage, but they were there. All *Torbay* wanted to do, having no torpedoes left, was to go home. But *Torbay* was close up against the coast of Zea island, and the destroyers barred the escape route.

Jim Sherwood recalls that we considered blowing up the submarine and seeking refuge ashore. This must have been partially misunderstood mess-deck gossip. There was a routine for scuttling the submarine, but no such drastic measure could have been contemplated without the first lieutenant's knowledge, nor would Miers have omitted such a crisis from his official report. All we needed to do was to be patient until they got bored and went away.

Eventually they did, or so we thought. Even so, on the way east on the surface that night, Jim, as port forward look-out, reported a destroyer right ahead. *Torbay* dived, and the destroyer passed by, suspecting nothing.

By now *Torbay* had no torpedoes and only nineteen rounds of 4-inch ammunition, so she headed for Alexandria. On the way, in the central Aegean, she passed close to two merchant ships escorted by one destroyer; but there was little future in trying to engage with what we had. Even so, had the destroyer not been there, Miers certainly would have.

One Italian U-boat, one tanker, one merchant vessel, and eight schooner/caiques had been sunk. Four patrol vessels and thirty-six aircraft had been encountered; eighty-one depth-charges had been experienced.

Captain Raw put in a list of recommendations for honours and awards; these came through in October. The Commander-in-Chief, Sir Andrew Cunningham, commented: 'A brilliantly conducted patrol. Lieutenant-Commander Miers is an outstanding Commanding Officer.'

7 Fourth Patrol – Gulf of Sirte and Crete

Torbay's folboteer and the Cretan Dunkirk

This patrol was from 2 to 28 August.

On this patrol we had just one folboteer, George Bremner, by now a sergeant. Of course, it was in accordance with Murphy's, or Sod's, Law that on this occasion we could have done with a cricket team of them, and in their primary role; not that Roger Courtney would have risked so many of his precious 'Basques in one exit'. In similar Murphy's Law fashion, *Torbay* was to have a doctor embarked when she did not need one, and not when she did.

Torbay was assigned Benghazi and eastwards. A close periscope reconnaissance of Ras Hilal and of Apollonia was carried out on 8 August, but there was nothing doing. On the 9th a hospital ship left Benghazi, bound probably for Italy. There was considerable doubt about the bona fides of these hospital ships, and if they were not illuminated at night we were instructed to sink them. *Torbay* made chase with a view to boarding to find out exactly what she carried; but the project aborted as *Torbay* had to dive to avoid an aircraft.

On the 10th five anti-submarine trawlers were observed patrolling in and around the searched channel leading to Benghazi; this was a sign that something might be expected and, sure enough, on the 12th *Torbay* attacked a convoy of two merchant ships escorted by one destroyer, one motor anti-submarine boat and one flying boat. One merchant ship was hit. The flying boat managed to lob a bomb fairly close, but not close enough.

On the 14th *Torbay* reconnoitred Benghazi, from the surface at dawn; but we could distinguish nothing worth making an enemy report. Course was then set for Crete, where *Torbay* was booked for a 'Special Operation'. This turned out to be rather more special than we had imagined.

The passage was made mainly on the surface, diving as necessary to avoid aircraft, and for one other reason. On the 15th in mid afternoon a U-boat, thought to be German, surfaced about five miles ahead and to the north. She was heading roughly south. Here one may note that she would not have surfaced had she seen *Torbay* through her periscope. But five miles is a long way for a small target through a periscope. *Torbay* dived with a view to doing a repeat *Jantina*. But the U-boat had apparently also seen *Torbay*, and she too dived. *Torbay* surfaced some forty minutes later for a good look around, but there was nothing in sight, so she dived again. At 1630 we got a fleeting glimpse through our periscope of the U-boat periscope – in fact, both of them. That, however was the final contact. *Torbay* surfaced at 2100 and made an enemy report in the hope that someone else might catch her, and then patrolled slowly around until midnight; nothing was seen or heard, so course was resumed for Crete.

Thinking in retrospect, *Torbay* and the U-boat were like two boxers: each could knock out the other. Yet such was our confidence that we were merely annoyed that we could not find her. The idea that she might torpedo *Torbay* crossed nobody's mind.

On reaching the area of Crete, *Torbay* disposed of a schooner, using first the gun and then demolition charges at 2140 on 16 August.

The operation, which turned out to be more than expected, was to land and later recover a certain Lieutenant-Commander Pool RNR. He was a Special Service officer who had made certain arrangements when he had been landed in Crete in July. He had, for example, directed evaders – that is, people who had avoided being rounded up into prisoner-of-war camps – to go to Preveli Monastery in south-western Crete. Pool's mission was to get in touch with resistance elements and to deliver stores, including a wireless transmitter, and certain instructions. Our friends in Crete had been warned to expect him, when and roughly where.

On the morning of the 18th *Torbay* dived north-west of Paximadia island off the south-west part of Crete. Conditions were bad, with half a gale blowing from the north. The daylight was spent reconnoitring the beaches through the periscope; in this our folboteer, George Bremner, took a considerable part.

After dark, at 2100, the prearranged signal from the shore was seen, and we launched Bremner, who was to make the first contact. The conditions, as Bremner had pointed out, were adverse in the extreme. The wind lifted the bow of the folbot, and the sergeant was swept away to seawards, for all his frantic paddling. Miers and Bremner had a heated argument prior to the launch, which may be said to have been against Bremner's better judgement. Even so, Miers' reaction was immediate. The first lieutenant was on the casing, preparing for the next stage of the operation; the order he got was, 'Secure everything; we are going after him; we would lose a good man there.' *Torbay* pursued and recovered Bremner. Then *Torbay* moved even closer inshore and launched Bremner for the second time. This time he made the beach, but not until about 2300, and by back-paddling, a relatively slow and exhausting method.

Meanwhile Pool had set off at 2230.

Back in due course, via Bremner, came an Australian sergeant and a New Zealand soldier. The Australian advised that there were plenty of Commonwealth troops in the vicinity; he volunteered to return ashore and muster a party for *Torbay* to rescue the following night. Bremner meanwhile had made contact with Cretans and asked them to spread the buzz that there might be a trip to

Egypt, means unspecified, available the following night. Bremner came back to *Torbay* at 0130 on the 19th, and *Torbay* withdrew to seaward to charge her batteries.

At 2215 on the 19th *Torbay* nosed in to the shore until she grounded gently. Then the first lieutenant flooded extra ballast in forward to hold the bow firmly down. Bremner went to the beach again, and he brought off Pool at 0015 on the 20th. Pool, who stayed with us to go back to Egypt, said that there were some twenty-eight awaiting evacuation and that there could be about another hundred if *Torbay* could come back for yet a third night. Even twenty-eight was more than Bremner could be expected to ferry one at a time; indeed, he was still exhausted after his ordeal the previous night.

So off went Bremner, with Tono Kidd, the engineer, towing a 'grass' or coir hawser. This has no great strength, but it has the merit of floating. The troops, except for the odd wounded, whom Bremner ferried, came out swimming alongside the grass or even hand over hand. *Torbay* blew ballast forward and backed off at 0255, having promised to come again for a third night.

To go back to the same place, and deliberately to ground, for yet another night may be deemed imprudent. Well, nothing venture, nothing gain. There must have been many more than a hundred people, including Cretans, who knew what was afoot. Cretans might have earned a good reward by betraying *Torbay*; but nobody did. Of course, one must take into account that the Resistance would have been ruthless should they have found out who had done it.

On the third night the signal from the shore was seen at 2108. Once again *Torbay* nosed in and grounded; once again the line was rigged to the shore, with the refinement that 'Mae West' inflated lifebelts were fastened to it at intervals. Close to one hundred came off that night; most came along the grass hawser, but the wounded via Bremner. One has been rather taking him for granted in this account, but let it be noted that on the third night alone he did thirty double journeys, *Torbay* to shore and back.

In February 1942 the following was published in the *London Gazette*:

MILITARY MEDAL

2880295 Sergeant George BREMNER
The Gordon Highlanders

From 1st August until December 1941 Sergeant Bremner has been engaged in three dangerous operations in connection with the rescue of British troops from enemy territory. On all occasions his coolness and courage contributed largely to the success of these hazardous operations.

When *Torbay* approached the beach for the third night, it could be seen from the bridge that there were quite some goings-on in the village on shore. It was not exactly farewell parties, but there were lights and there were dogs barking. George Bremner, from his folbot at sea-level, could not see this; that was just as well, as it might have worried him. With hindsight, one may judge that the Resistance had taken steps to ensure that no motorized German patrol would get to the area that night. Communications in southern Crete were rudimentary at the best of times, and trees may fall across roads in stormy weather.

By 2330 on the 20th it was over. *Torbay* backed off and sailed. She did a trim dive at dawn to ensure that ballasting had been adjusted to the presence of nearly 140 extra people weighing perhaps eleven stone each.

The helpful monks from Preveli Monastery had meanwhile driven their goats up and down the beach to obliterate traces of the evacuation.

In May 1985 a bronze tablet was put in the abbey of Preveli, Crete. In Greek and English it says: 'This Tablet commemorates the deep gratitude of the British, New Zealand, and Australian servicemen befriended by the Monks of Preveli Monastery and Cretans from surrounding villages, who, at great personal risk, helped them to escape by British Submarines during the dark days of 1941.'

The official record of the rescue shows a total of 130, but this does not include Pool and his party. We got thirteen officers and 117 other ranks. One hundred and twenty-one were Commonwealth, of whom sixty-two were New Zealanders. There were eight Greeks and one Yugoslav. At one stage we had considerably more Greeks but, when the Commonwealth numbers awaiting became apparent, we had to disappoint them and send them back ashore, either swimming or via Bremner. Throughout the evacuations from Greece and Crete it was standing instructions that Commonwealth troops must have priority.

Lieutenant-Commander Pool, whose part in *Torbay*'s fourth patrol was only the 'tip of his iceberg', was awarded the Distinguished Service Order in early November 1941.

When taking the ground on the second night, *Torbay* went in very gently; even so, she was unlucky in that she must have lodged on some protuberance. It punctured the staybrite steel cage, at the front of the keel, in which lived the Sonar oscillator. This was a pity, but the gains were well worth the damage. Besides that, after getting back to Alexandria, *Torbay* had to go to Port Said to dock for repairs, there being a queue for the Alexandria docks. At Port Said Campbell and Chapman made friends with a Muscovy Duck, as described in Chapter 11. They would not have wanted to miss that.

One hundred and thirty soldiers, one merchant ship and one schooner on the account; also what amounted to at least three special operations. Even more important, in view of what was to follow, was the experience that *Torbay*'s casing party gained in the matter of launching and recovering folbots.

Much later the activities of what were, to the Germans, subversive elements in Crete did not pass without notice, to the extent that reprisals, such as the taking and execution of hostages, occurred. This caused Middle East headquarters to send to Crete two army officers, Patrick Leigh-Fermor and William Stanley Moss. Guided and aided by the Resistance and dressed in German uniforms, they kidnapped the German commandant, General

Kreipe. After a hair-raising game of hide-and-seek, they duly delivered Kreipe to GHQ Middle East in Cairo; there, no doubt, he was interrogated and given a good talking-to. The operation was designed to make subsequent commandants tread with care.*

A Ballad Of Crete

How could it be done?
By a Roman Catholic Son,
In August, Mediterranean Fleet,
Eleven weeks after,
Forgive our laughter,
The 'end' of the Battle of Crete?

Soldiers were some of intransigent stamp.
They would not go to prison camp.
They holed up with those friendly,
Such as the Monastery at Preveli.

Three nights, emerging from the flood,
Torbay called like any watery god,
'Come on, Cobbers, have no fear,
The bloody Royal Nivey's here.'

The monks
Were in abundance
Until, one day,
One was heard to say,
'Cobber, be of good cheer,
The bloody Royal Nivey's here.
So, don't get tight,
Sphakia beach, tonight.'

At that sound
The word got around,
From village to village,
From monk to priest,
Until at least
Even wounded were sound
Enough to reach
Sphakia beach.

* See *Ill Met By Moonlight* by W. Stanley Moss (Buchan & Enwright, 1985)

So, worry no more, Soldier,
Worry no more.
Leave poor old conquered Crete,
And head for Egypt's shore.
Safe in the *Torbay*, Soldier,
Cling to life no more.
Leave that poor old conquered Crete,
And live to fight more.

4th and 5th Patrols 1941

4th Patrol 2nd to 28th August 1941
5th Patrol 6th to 28th September 1941

Miles
0   200   400

N

TURKEY

BEIRUT

CYPRUS

PORT SAID

ALEXANDRIA

UB ESCAPED 7/9

MV 10/9

MV 19/9

Crete

EGYPT

RESCUE AREA 18,19,20/8

SCHOONER 16/8

UB ESCAPED 15/8

DERNA

TOBRUK

BENGHAZI

Cyrenaica

MV 12/8

GREECE

ATHENS

Peloponnese

MEDITERRANEAN SEA

ITALY

MESSINA

SICILY

MALTA

TARANTO

LIBYA

8   Fifth Patrol –
Crete, Aegean, Dardanelles

In which frustrations test the Torbay's *patience and a
doctor her eyes*

This patrol was from 6 to 28 September.

The night we sailed we passed, shortly before 2300, a
friendly force of cruisers and destroyers coming in. By this
time we knew well that no Italian surface force would be
within thirty miles of Alexandria. Even so, we had not
been warned.

It was the custom, because of the gradual deterioration of
torpedo mechanisms once immersed in salt water, not to
flood the tubes until reaching the patrol area. This was a
mistake, later corrected by revised procedures, because
you never know.

Torbay had proceeded on the surface during the night
and had dived at dawn. She was still far closer to Egypt
than to the patrol area; thus the tubes were not flooded. In
the case of internal tubes, they had to be flooded before
they could be fired. In the afternoon of the 7th Chapman,
on watch, called Miers because he thought he saw an
Italian U-boat on the surface. It was; and Miers ordered
that the six internal tubes be brought to the ready. But,
because they had first to be flooded, they were not ready
until after the opportunity to fire had passed. So what
about the 4-inch gun?

Torbay surfaced and made to open fire. The first round

was a misfire. After such an event, you are supposed to wait for thirty minutes before opening the breech; this is in case the propellant charge does a delayed explosion, known as 'cooking-off', killing or burning the gun's crew. However, the gun's crew did not hesitate to open the breech and seek to extract the dud round. But it was jammed in the breech and there was no more they could do at the time.

While this was going on, the Italian dived, shortly followed by *Torbay*. For the rest of the day we listened on the Sonar, in case we might pick her up by sound; this was unlikely anyway, and there were no indications. *Torbay* went slowly in the direction in which the enemy might be expected to go – that is, away from Alexandria, since she must know that she had been sighted and would be reported.

During the day Miers considered all options. We had one, repeat one, depth-charge; it was by the Asdic cabinet in the control room, which is amidships; its function was, in a scuttling situation, to destroy the Asdic circuitry lest it be captured and copied. The depth-charge was to be detonated by delay-action Bickford's fuse, not by hydrostatic depth mechanism; this was because, in the circumstances contemplated, the submarine might be in shallow water or even aground.

Miers' idea was that we should somehow trundle the depth-charge to the forward hatch; then surface and rig the torpedo derrick which was housed in the casing; then start the capstan and haul the depth-charge into the fresh air; then swing it outboard with an uncertain quantity of Bickford's fuse attached. Any time after surfacing, *Torbay* would be open to torpedo attack if the Italian was still near. As for the uncertain fuse length, how fast would the depth-charge sink? Exactly where and at what depth would the Italian be? Neither of these we would know; a submarine is not designed as a depth-charge dispenser.

It would usually take two or even three figures of depth-charges to sink a submarine, so what chance would there be with one? One thing stood out: when the depth-charge went off, the closest submarine to it would probably be *Torbay*. A plan born in haste, out of frustration and disappointment, may be flawed. At any rate, neither the first lieutenant nor the engineer officer would have anything to do with it; so Miers let the matter drop.

At dusk *Torbay* surfaced, cleared the jammed gun and readied it for action; it was the intention to try it again should the Italian by chance be seen. Some chance it was, indeed, an astronomical figure to one against. Then an orange moon started to rise over the horizon. Before the moon became a semi-circle, Chapman on the bridge saw the Italian silhouetted against it; so off we went at full speed on the engines. However, once the moon lifted clear of the horizon, we never saw that Italian again.

Miers was most put out. Said he, 'However well we may do, the fact is that we have missed a golden opportunity.' That was true, but there is a saying about spilt milk.

The occasion was not a unique misfire; there were others, and they were dealt with in the summary fashion described. Two mishaps *were* unique, the torpedoes not being ready in time, and the gun jamming. Here it may be mentioned that the ammunition we were using was very old stock; new was coming along, but not as fast as it was being used. Equally, some of the torpedoes we were given were very ancient Mark IVs instead of the Mark VIIIs we were supposed to have. Often we had a mixed bag, which made for difficulty: the Mark IV had been souped up to go at 40 knots like the Mark VIII, but it could not keep it up for so long, so that at any range above some 5,000 yards the Mark IV would start to tail off and fall behind, thus upsetting the spreading of the salvo.

On the 9th *Torbay* was instructed to go to Crete, Zea Channel, Doro Channel, then the Dardanelles. So it happened that in the morning of the 10th two merchant ships, escorted by a torpedo boat, were seen bound to the east from Suda Bay. *Torbay* was approaching a good firing-position but was at the last minute thwarted by having to go deep to avoid the torpedo boat. When she had passed, the attack was resumed, but by this time on a very broad and unfavourable track. It was calm, and when the torpedoes were fired, the enemy saw the approaching tracks and 'combed' them – that is they steered a parallel course towards or away. The result was no hits.

Miers considered whither the group would be going. Rhodes or Candia, in eastern Crete, seemed probable. It also seemed that, by a surface dash, we might catch up at dusk or soon after. Consequently the afternoon was spent bobbing up and down like a yoyo, as *Torbay* crash-dived for aircraft in between runs at full speed on the surface. Miers was a little upset when he found that the first lieutenant had been running the air compressors whilst on the surface; but it was pointed out that all the up and down had caned the high-pressure air far more than the batteries.

By 1717 *Torbay* was off Candia, and it was decided to inspect this closely from submerged. There were three merchant ships. The one to seaward, probably one of those we had missed earlier, could be attacked by a torpedo fired through the harbour entrance. She was duly torpedoed at about 2000 in the last of the dusk. Soon afterwards, *Torbay* surfaced to make a get-away; she was only about a mile and a half from Candia lighthouse, was seen and fired upon by 20- or 40-millimetre cannon. Down went *Torbay*, and tried again some ten minutes later, only to be again put down by the approach of an aircraft. A third attempt, at 2032, was successful, and course was set for the Zea Channel.

Nothing was encountered in the Zea and Doro Channels, and *Torbay* reached the Dardanelles on the 13th. She took up position close to Cape Helles, as in the second patrol. On the 13th and 14th two possible targets were pursued, but they turned out to be Turkish and so had to be left alone. *Torbay* was then ordered to the Gulf of Athens, which was reached on the 16th.

The Gulf of Athens has a relatively wide approach, compared, for example, with the Dardanelles. The close approaches to Piraeus, the port of Athens, were known to be littered with defensive minefields. One had therefore to stay out in the relative deep field, some ten to twenty miles north-east of San Giorgio island. The enemy there had a wide choice of routes, and the very limited mobility of a submerged submarine meant that it was impossible to cover all of them. The operating authority might have done better to put us in the Zea, Thermia or Kithera Channels.

Sure enough, in the dawn of the 17th three merchant ships with escorts were seen; but they passed well out of torpedo range, which was of the order of four miles. The rest of the morning was spent keeping out of the way of a flotilla of mine-sweepers doing a searching sweep for mines. We did not wish them to snag their sweeps on *Torbay*.

On the 18th a gun action against a small merchant ship was contemplated, but a patrolling aircraft made it impracticable. Later, in the afternoon, one merchant ship, escorted by two destroyers and an aircraft, appeared. An enemy alteration of course put *Torbay* too fine on the bow and thus too close off track to fire. The standard measure was to go deep and run out at full speed to open the range. The forward hydroplanes chose this moment to jam in the hard to rise position. The first lieutenant kept *Torbay* from doing a salmon leap to the surface by using 'Q' tank, which had to be flooded and blown twice before the hydroplanes were under control in manual operation. When order was restored, the opportunity to attack had passed.

In the afternoon of the 19th *Torbay* met two merchant ships, an armed merchant cruiser and two destroyers. One merchant ship was struck, and *Torbay* was favoured with fourteen fairly unpleasant depth-charges. A further attack was carried out on a fairly small target on the 21st, ten miles north of San Giorgio island. The torpedoes ran under, probably because *Torbay* was too close, so that they had not taken up their set depth before crossing the target line. Another eleven depth-charges were *Torbay*'s only reward.

On the 22nd the tanker *Tarvisio*, escorted by two destroyers and two aircraft, was seen passing out of range. Clearly, after what had happened in *Torbay*'s second and third patrols, the enemy were trying to look after their tankers in the Aegean. Nothing further was seen, and *Torbay* reached Alexandria without incident.

On this patrol we had Surgeon Lieutenant Jones with us. He was monitoring health in general, and eyesight and night vision in particular. All the officers of the watch and ratings employed on look-out duty were eye-tested at intervals. It was found that performance did fall away; whether this was owing to diet, lack of exercise, or bad atmosphere is not clear. Of course, for the officers of the watch and look-outs, eyes are not the whole story. The interpreting brain behind the eyes is a vital factor. Is that just a patch of darker cloud or is it the dim outline of a ship in the mist? Those with the best eyesight were not always the best look-outs.

Of course the look-outs were conscientious; they knew that our lives depended on them, and they usually saw objects first. They did an hour, or less, at a time on the bridge. The officer of the watch, on the other hand, did a two-hour stint. There were four look-outs, each with a 90-degree sector to monitor, and with no other duties. The officer of the watch, though, was in receipt of information from, and had to give instructions to, the control room down below, where the helmsman was connected to the bridge by a voice pipe. As regards looking out, when other things allowed, the officer of the watch had a roving commission.

But it did happen that, in misty conditions at night in the Dardanelles area, the officer of the watch was the first to note a suspicious blur. In this order, he turned end on, stopped the engines, called the captain and instructed Sonar to listen on the bearing. When *Torbay*'s self noise stopped, Sonar was able to hear high revving turbine hydrophone effect. It was an Italian destroyer passing on its way; and it did.

If the officer of the watch had got this sort of routine wrong, he would have got into trouble with Miers and with the first lieutenant in his capacity as senior watchkeeper. But in this case the foregoing was hardly likely, because the officer of the watch *was* the first lieutenant.

The doctor discovered something which Chapman already knew, because Miers had told him. This was that Miers had one good eye and one not so good; one eye was 'master', and the other a sometimes laggard slave. Judging distance is easier with two synchronized eyes than with just one; that is why the brilliant England goalkeeper Gordon Banks had to pack it in when he lost an eye in an accident.

Miers had managed to conceal the problem from the relatively rudimentary medical examination for entry to the Royal Navy in the 1920s; he would otherwise have been accepted only into the engineering or paymaster branches. The older submarines had monocular periscopes only, so that Miers was quite at home using his master eye. *Torbay*, on the other hand, had one binocular periscope, with high power magnification, and one slim monocular one, with no magnification. One would use the latter in the closing stages of an attack, because the difference in what one was poking above the water may be compared with a walking-stick or telegraph pole. When using the binocular periscope, Miers tended to use it as if it were monocular; this explained why he had not at once appreciated the collision situation described in Chapter 3.

Even so, Miers was proficient at rugger and at tennis and was quite a good wicket-keeper at cricket; here the thumps on his legs may have precipitated his varicose veins.

There came a time when Chapman wished they had lent us a doctor on a patrol later than this one.

Two merchant ships, twenty-five depth-charges, fifty-two hostile aircraft sightings, twenty-two patrol vessels and a lot of frustration caused by both procedural and material problems.

6th and 7th Patrols 1941

6th Patrol 7th to 18th October 1941

7th Patrol 10th to 24th November 1941

Miles

0   50   100

N

MEDITERRANEAN SEA

Crete

LIBYA

Cyrenaica

EGYPT

ALEXANDRIA

EL ALAMEIN

TOBRUK

ZAVIET EL HAMANA

BEDA LITTORIA

RAS HILAL

DERNA

APOLLONIA

LANDING 10/10

AIRCRAFT 20/11

AIRCRAFT HANGAR 15/10

LANDING 14/11

9   Sixth and Seventh Patrols – Gulf of Sirte, Beda Littoria

We launch a commando raid behind Rommel's lines and shoot up an aircraft (on the ground)

The sixth patrol was from 7 to 18 October; the seventh was from 10 to 24 November.

Both were in aid of a Special Operation; this was to land the Scottish commando behind Rommel's lines, to create havoc to command and control, at a date to coincide with the opening of General Sir Alan Cunningham's Western Desert offensive known as 'Operation Crusader'. It was also hoped, by some of the more ambitious, to capture or kill General Rommel the legendary leader of the German Afrika Korps.*

Such was the importance attached to this gambit that *Torbay* and her sister submarine *Talisman* were withdrawn from the normal operational cycle for five weeks. Miers was probably in the know from the start, but for security reasons the rest of *Torbay* knew not much until we had sailed from Alexandria for the seventh patrol.

Captain Haselden was the *sine qua non* of the whole operation. He had served in local forces in Cyrenaica; he could pass for a Senussi Arab, and he spoke Arabic fluently. His was the reconnaissance that made the operation feasible; his intervention, when the commandos

---

* The operation has been described in *SBS in World War II* and also in a book about the late Lieutenant-Colonel Geoffrey Keyes VC. So far as is known, it has not been written up from the submarine point of view.

landed thirty-four-strong instead of fifty-six, meant that the list of targets needed not quite so heavily to be pruned. Sadly Haselden, by then a lieutenant-colonel, was killed in 1942 in the abortive raid on Tobruk after Rommel had captured the latter.

Having sailed on 7 October, *Torbay* spent the day of the 10th doing a periscope reconnaissance of the area variously called Ras el Hamama or Zaviet el Hamama, seventeen miles west of Apollonia. This was to be the eventual landing-place for the commando, but this had not yet been settled.

After dark that day, Corporal Severn with his folbot was readied. Captain Haselden had an Arab companion and a considerable load of stores. One passenger plus stores was all that Severn could manage on one trip; so, to save Severn making two, with the submarine meanwhile hanging about close inshore, Haselden elected to swim. He had a watertight torch with which to signal his safe arrival, but otherwise he was naked, so that any German or Italian reception committee on the beach would not learn much from his 'uniform'.

In those days Alexandria had no such thing as a waterproof torch. In this, and in earlier and later operations, *Torbay* achieved waterproofing by enclosing the torch in a condom.

Severn, with Arab and stores, set off, followed by Haselden, who swam the roughly 300 yards to the beach in twelve minutes. Severn was back and his boat recovered and struck down below, and the total time was thirty-four minutes from start to finish. *Torbay* had indeed profited from the experience in the fourth patrol.

Soon after the landing, Alexandria had news of a convoy, with cruisers and destroyers, apparently heading for Benghazi. On the 11th *Torbay* was ordered out 'into the blue' some 120 miles north of Benghazi. As has been inferred before, being out in the blue is not much good for a World War II submersible. Yet it was done over and again. A focal point is the answer: why not Benghazi? On the 13th Miers moved to a position some forty miles north of Benghazi. That was more like it, but nothing was seen, and soon afterwards *Torbay* was recalled.

Torbay had had a good look at Apollonia during a previous patrol and had noted a large aircraft hangar. It seemed that this might be improved by some 4-inch shells. So in the evening of the 15th *Torbay* opened fire; three hits were observed before shells from shore batteries made it prudent to dive away.

Meanwhile Captain Haselden was also homeward bound, to Cairo by camel rather like an old Jack Hulbert film.

During the period between the sixth and seventh patrols, various rehearsals were carried out. As a preliminary, the first lieutenant was told that he would have to accommodate two folbots, each with crews of two, fourteen rubber boats and twenty-eight heavily armed commandos. These latter were to be landed at a secret destination, but it was not hard to judge where.

This was not like an evacuation, as from Crete, when landing chaps in one piece was good enough. These people had to be landed well fed, in the pink of condition and with their morale high. The removal of the six reload torpedoes, and the conversion of the racks into comfortable bunks, went a long way towards solving the sleeping-problem; and, of course, the commandos were welcome to any unoccupied bunk or hammock. If the watchkeeper, coming off watch, found his place taken, he merely moved into the slot recently occupied by his relief, a system known as 'hot bunking'.

What about feeding, washing, lavatories, arms and ammunition stowage? All were relatively small problems readily solved.

The folbots and the rubber boats had to be dismantled or collapsed. The assembly of folbots below, with the midships frame adjusted on the casing, has already been explained. The rubber boats came up in parcels, each with a pair of bellows; it was astonishing what a noise fourteen pairs of bellows, all puffing at once, seemed to make. But on the night the weather was so bad that that was quite unimportant.

Talisman was to accompany *Torbay*, under command of *Torbay* and with a similar passenger load. In the end it was settled as *Torbay*, Lieutenant-Colonel Keyes plus twenty-seven, *Talisman*, Lieutenant-Colonel Laycock (in overall command Scottish commando) plus twenty-seven.

There is a school of thought which says that this should not have been, for the whole, sometimes unhappy, history of Combined Operations has pointed to the importance of co-location of the officer commanding troops and the senior officer afloat. Unfortunately in this case personalities may have led to disregard of military prudence. What would have happened if Middle East headquarters in receipt of up-to-date Intelligence from air reconnaissance, agents and other sources, had wanted to make some changes? Say, the place of landing, say the date of landing. Then OC Troops and SO afloat could communicate only by a protracted procedure. This was because *Torbay* and *Talisman* sailed separately and independently and were not in direct communication until rendezvous off Zaviet el Hamama.

This would have been the way of it had Miers wanted to talk to Laycock. *Torbay* would pass a ciphered message, on high-frequency radio, to the first shore wireless station which answered her call. The shore wireless station would then pass the message to Rugby wireless station, which had a very powerful low-frequency transmitter on sixteen kilocycles (now called kilohertz). Rugby would retransmit not just once but several times, so that *Talisman* would in due course get it; this was because submarines could hear Rugby even when submerged and were enjoined to listen at a number of routine periods throughout the twenty-four hours. *Talisman* could reply by the same devious route.

All the same, intercommunication would have been measured at least in hours, and possibly in days. Moreover, two submarines calling on high-frequency radio close to the North African coast might well have alerted the enemy to the fact that something unusual and untoward was afoot.

The split command also led to a non-event which will be

described later.

Talisman had been to have a look at an alternative landing-place called Ras Hilal. Three SBS and one Scottish commando were landed on 24 October. They did not come back and were reported as being prisoners near Derna. It was assumed that Ras Hilal might well be compromised, so it was discarded.

Soon after sailing on 10 November, *Torbay* did the routine trim dive during which, as normal, all compartments were asked to check for leaks and report. Of course, the answer 'No' was expected. By this time we knew the importance of our mission, so it was horrifying to hear Tono Kidd report, 'Yes, we have a hole in the hull about under the muffler tanks.' These were tanks external to the hull through which passed the diesel engine exhausts, through a water bath to muffle the sound. The hole was smartly filled with a wooden plug with a shoring arrangement behind it.

But if the hull had worn into a hole, how thin was the plating around the hole? What would happen if we were depth-charged? Would the plug pop out and the hole get bigger? More than that, Miers had considerable reservations about even going deep; so he ordered eighty feet, to see what would happen. The repair held; we would go on.

So far so good; but *Torbay*, in between landing and hopefully re-embarking the commandos, was supposed to join the rough-and-tumble off Benghazi. This we were not in a position to do, and Alexandria must be told. But if we told the whole holey truth, we would almost certainly be recalled, and the commando force would at once be halved. Miers' solution was to send a deliberately corrupt ciphered signal: 'Will be unable to patrol after landing because of defective bananas.' 'Bananas' was a mistake for 'hull'. Try it as a crossword clue, Alexandria.

Torbay and *Talisman* were off Zaviet el Hamama at dusk on 14 November, and *Torbay* closed the beach first. The conditions were most unfavourable, with sea and swell rolling in from the north-east. But there was no way that Operation Crusader could be delayed just because a few commandos were not in position. They knew it, we knew it, the attempt had to be made; and there was the pre-arranged signal on the beach from Haselden. This time David Stirling's Long Range Desert Group had brought him most of the way.

Torbay sent in a folbot to talk to Haselden and started preparing the party with their rubber boats on the forward casing. The first lieutenant instructed the soldiers, as soon as their boats were inflated, to sit in them. When the sea came over, they were to grind their arses into the boat's bottom whilst bearing up with their arms against the wire jackstay, which ran at a suitable height from *Torbay's* bow to the gun tower. Even so, we lost four boats overboard during the preparations. Leading Seaman Hammond and Able Seaman Vine swam after them and brought them back. The gear inside had been secured, so that nothing was lost.

At 2130 the launch of the rubber boats started. *Torbay's* casing party lowered the boats to the water and towed them, one at a time, to the forward hydroplanes, whence the commandos had been shown how to board. But that was in the calm waters of a remote, for secrecy, part of the huge harbour of Alexandria. On the night, in the sea and swell, it was much more difficult, and boat after boat capsized as rather inexperienced soldiers tried to board. Then into the sea went Vine, or Hammond, or both, righted the boat and brought it back into position. What was about an hour in rehearsal took four.

By half past midnight, *Torbay* had got thirteen pairs of soldiers safely away, and they made the shore guided by the folbots. One of the final pair, during a capsize, had crushed a leg between his boat and the submarine. He and his partner wanted to try again, in fact for the third time, but Miers would not allow it. The injured man could not march and would be a burden on the rest. Besides this, *Torbay* had already spent much longer than planned off the landing-beach, and there was *Talisman*, with a full outfit of twenty-eight commandos, waiting. *Torbay* and *Talisman* had been in communication by infra-red signal lamps; *Torbay* withdrew having called *Talisman* to come in.

She had been 'keeping cave' to seaward for *Torbay*, and we did the same for her. Miers had to be on the bridge during the launch operation, keeping the submarine in position, talking to *Talisman* and to the folbots, and so on, but he could see what was going on. Of the casing party in general, he reported, 'There were occasions when I doubted their physical strength to carry the operation to a successful conclusion'; of the first lieutenant he said, '... so little did he spare himself that he was, at the end, reduced to a state of physical exhaustion from which he took several days to recover.'

That was about right; Chapman kept going and stood his watches with the aid of judicious doses of a stimulant drug called Benzedrine. Like all stimulants, it was relatively short-lived, and it left one in a worse state than when first the drug was taken. Benzedrine was not a service issue, but both Campbell and Chapman had private supplies. Different people needed different doses, and it was wise to experiment, at a time when it did not matter, to find out the appropriate dose. Campbell's dose was four tablets, whilst Chapman's was two; but then Campbell was a larger person. In the case of one officer, he steadily increased his dose to six tablets, still with no effect, so Chapman advised him to stop; clearly his body chemistry merely rejected Benzedrine, as opposed to reacting to it.

It is appropriate to say a little more about one of *Torbay*'s casing party that night, Able Seaman James Sydney Vine (to be DSM). The book *The Distinguished Service Medal, 1939-1946** refers to Vine and his colleague Able Seaman Hammond: 'They had both shown outstanding courage and were completely exhausted at the finish. Vine in particular was badly bruised and battered, injured in the head, and had his back cut by boat ropes; however, nothing would persuade him to go below for medical attention until the last boat was successfully launched ... Commander Miers reported: "The seamanlike qualities he displayed were all the more remarkable considering that he was a

---

* Compiled and edited by W.H. Fevyer (J.B. Hayward & Son, Polstead, Suffolk).

Kentish market gardener by trade – in fact a 'Hostilities Only' man, and the *Torbay* was his first Submarine''.'

Talisman realized that the whole affair was running late, and decided to take an unusual measure – to put her bow on the ground, as had *Torbay* off Crete. In the different circumstances this was a mistake, to be compounded by another. With the heavily flooded bow firmly aground, the stern rose to the incoming sea and swell, whereas the bow did not. Thus a surge of sea over the forward casing swept away half the commandos, plus boats. What made it worse, bearing in mind that the soldiers were bearing up on the jackstay, was that the latter carried away under the strain; it might not have been inspected all that recently.

Now for the sad mistake. *Torbay* had learnt by experiment that the commandos, equipped with extra ammunition, grenades and personal arms slung around the person, were very heavy. It took not one Mae West lifebelt to keep a man afloat, it needed two. *Talisman* had not found this out. *Torbay*'s soldiers who went overboard floated; *Talisman*'s sank. Chapman must share the blame for this mistake, rather an expensive one; he should have made sure that *Talisman*'s first lieutenant knew the score.

In the end *Talisman* withdrew at 0400 on the 15th, having succeeded in landing Laycock plus seven. In view of the very considerable reduction in the force ashore, Miers decided there was no point in keeping two submarines waiting for the planned re-embarkation. *Torbay* got in touch with *Talisman* by supersonic underwater telegraphy at noon on the 15th and ordered her home.

For this brief account of the operation ashore the writer is indebted to the official report of General Sir Robert Laycock, and to Captain Haselden, whom he met in Cairo after the event.

The original plan had three groups of targets around Beda Littoria, Cirene and Apollonia. The list had to be carved down in view of the diminution of the force, but Haselden and his friends volunteered to take on a few targets. In the result, the German HQ and 'the

Commander-in-Chief's House' were attacked at Beda Littoria, as were communications installations, a petrol distribution point and an electric light plant, south of Cirene. It was hoped that the Beda Littoria targets included Rommel's HQ and house. It was later discovered that this was not so; Rommel was not there nor ever had been; Intelligence had got it wrong.

Laycock stayed at the commando-improvised HQ near the beach. Unwanted gear, such as boats, was hidden, and the attack parties went their ways.

Keyes led the Beda Littoria party with, amongst others, a Captain Campbell and a Sergeant Terry. Unfortunately they had to put down a sentry outside the HQ with a shot; only a single shot, but enough to disturb the wasps' nest. Then Sergeant Terry had to fire a burst of tommy-gun up the stairs to the first floor, to discourage people from coming down. At this point Keyes opened the door of a darkened room and fell in a hail of bullets. Sergeant Terry emptied two tommy-gun magazines into the room; then Captain Campbell rolled in a grenade and slammed the door; it might have been wiser to have done this in the first place.

Keyes was carried outside, where he died almost at once. By this time there was firing all over the place, and Captain Campbell was wounded by a stray bullet; he could not walk, so he ordered Terry to leave him to give himself up.

In the end all except Laycock, Haselden and Terry were killed or captured. The three made it back to Cairo, but over land; *Torbay* brought nobody back, apart from the two who had not landed, as will be explained.

The 18th and 19th had been appointed for re-embarkation and there was an alternative beach. *Torbay* approached the primary beach and established communication with Laycock. The cache had been discovered, and they needed lifebelts, food and water. Miers suggested that they should swim off to *Torbay*, because it was still blowing from the north in such a way that a rubber boat could not succeed, even if they had any. The suggestion was declined, so

Torbay sent an unmanned rubber boat to drift before the wind with the required stores. Miers judged nicely where to launch, and the boat came ashore within twenty yards of where Laycock was standing. Having agreed to return the next night, *Torbay* withdrew.

On the 19th periscope reconnaissance of the beach showed no activity, but in fact the shore party were discovered that day and split up for a *sauve qui peut*. They might have done better to try swimming with the lifebelts we had sent in. It resulted that there were no signals from shore that night. *Torbay* sent in a folbot to reconnoitre but nobody was found. *Torbay* then moved to the alternative beach and drew another blank.

The operation orders had specified the two evacuation beaches, primary and secondary. After sailing from Alexandria, a group of Laycock's party had made a private arrangement with *Talisman* for yet a third evacuation beach. What is wrong with this is that there was absolutely nothing right about it: there is no room in war for private arrangements. *Torbay*, senior officer afloat, did not even know; nor did *Talisman* own up when ordered home; she had ample opportunity, for she and *Torbay* were in good and secure communication on the 15th. There could have been people at this third beach, though, since so few of *Talisman*'s soldiers actually got ashore, this is improbable.

The matter came to light in harbour at Alexandria. An officer, deeply upset about the whole thing, confided in Chapman and asked what he could do. Chapman replied, 'You have done all that you can, you have told me; this is a matter for Miers, but I shall not remember whence I got the rumour. You, now, just do a Brer Rabbit: lie low and say nuffin.'

Miers went off like a 5 November squib; so, having lit the blue touchpaper, Chapman retired hastily to let him get on with it. There was no mention of the third beach in any of the official reports; and it was not to be long before *Talisman* took her secrets to the bottom of the Mediterranean.

On the 20th the two beaches were black with Italians

and there was air reconnaissance to seaward. According to Haselden, two killed or captured commandos had marked their maps, a thing they were expressly forbidden to do. By noon on the 21st Miers decided to abandon hope and go home; but first, what about that air reconnaissance? It was by a light aircraft of low endurance, so that several times a day he had to land for fuel. *Torbay* had always taken a bearing when he disappeared behind the sandhills to land. As these bearings were from many different positions, we could pinpoint the landing-strip. It was well within gun range from close inshore.

At half past three the aircraft was on the ground, and up came *Torbay*. The gun's crew, being at a level lower than the bridge, could not see the target, so we told them to aim at anything, so long as it was the same thing, and we ordered corrections, left and right, up and down, from the bridge. The aircraft flew no more that day, nor, probably, any other day. That was most satisfactory; the continual presence of the aircraft, in the by-now calm conditions, meant that we were hardly ever able to blow the heads – that is, to discharge excrement overboard, so that the submarine had been filling with that and resentment.

Torbay's part in the landing may be judged a success, *Talisman*'s less so. According to Haselden, three staff officers 'better than majors' were killed at Beda Littoria. A lot of damage was done near Cirene. The Inspector General Polizia Africana Italiana advised special vigilance in all rear areas. No doubt a lot of unfortunates finished up on dull sentry duty instead of chianti in the canteen. Moreover, it was the only occasion when an aircraft was shot up on the ground by a submarine.

10   Eighth Patrol –
Crete, Navarin

In which one Torbay *torpedo misses its mark* –
Torbay *herself – but others strike home*

This patrol was from 9 to 27 December.

Embarked was a Captain Wilson of the Special Boat Section. His folbot mission was to be offence, rather than reconnaissance or agent-landing. He had limpet mines; these are like sections of a sphere, with strong magnets on the flat side, so that they cling to the hull of a steel ship on or below the water line. The part-spherical profile meant that they would probably still cling even if the vessel got under way; they had a delay-action fuse. In the event Wilson was not successful.

A close periscope reconnaissance of Suda Bay was carried out on the 12th. There were a tanker, three merchant ships, a corvette and three anti-submarine trawlers. All were well tucked away behind an anti-submarine and anti-torpedo boom, so *Torbay* had to be content with sinking a schooner laden with petrol or oil drums.

On the 13th *Torbay* moved to Navarin in the Peloponnese, and Methoni, which is six miles further south. In the vicinity was the large minelaying submarine *Porpoise*; she had vacated the billet in favour of *Torbay* and was within a few days of the end of her patrol. Very likely she was needed to do another run with stores and fuel to beleaguered Malta; this had for some time been a priority

96

Commander Tony Miers,
early 1942

Sergeant George Bremner of
the London Scottish
(Gordon Highlanders), autumn 1941

A supply ship getting the gun off
Corfu during the tenth patrol, March
1942

Torbay's crew in February 1942

Torbay leaving Alexandria, bound for home, May 1942; and
Chapman, the first lieutenant *(insert)*, February 1942

Some of the First Submarine Flotilla at Alexandria in February 1942. In the second row from the front are seated Captain 'Sammy' Raw (sixth from the left) and Commander John Wallace Linton (fourth from the right)

In May 1942, Commander-in-Chief Sir Henry Pridham-Wippell came to say goodbye and safe home

Admiral Vian goes below, May 1942 (Captain Guy Grantham and Sub-Lieutenant Tony Melville-Ross are in the left background)

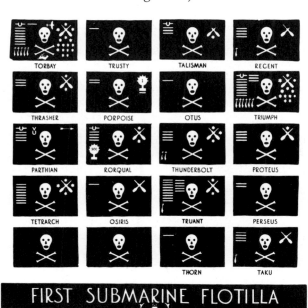

First Submarine Flotilla Jolly Rogers at the end of 1941

Torbay in home waters, early 1941

Torbay was modified for her second commission; during the refit, air warning radar and an oerlikon gun were fitted

Admiral Sir Max Horton with Miers at the Connaught Rooms,
London

At Buckingham Palace. Left to right: Chapman, Kidd,
Verschoyle-Campbell and Miers

'Torbays' at Buckingham Palace in July 1942 after receiving decorations from King George VI. From left to right: Leading Stoker Bennett, Engine Room Artificer Collins, Petty Officer Rayner, Leading Stoker Webb, Stoker Petty Officer Monk, Leading Seaman Hammond, Chief Stoker Skerrat, Able Seaman Vine, Lieutenant Kidd, Leading Seaman Guinelly, Lieutenant Chapman, Chief Engine-room Artificer Pinch, Commander Miers,

Electrical Artificer Rintoul, Lieutenant Verschoyle-Campbell, Petty Officer Kember, Leading Stoker Jones, Stoker Petty Officer Belcher, Chief Petty Officer Baker, Leading Seaman Cusator, Petty Officer Armishaw, Petty Officer Jefferson, Stoker Conaty, Able Seaman Gavin, Petty Officer Batten, Petty Officer Telegraphist Clark, Leading Signalman Maclean and Leading Seaman Phillips task for *Porpoise*. The two submarines spoke to each other by supersonic underwater telegraphy at intervals until *Porpoise* left on the 16th.

Porpoise had torpedoed a merchant ship, the *Andrea Gritti*, and she was beached at Methoni. But she could be salved and she needed to be finished off. One possibility was to send in Captain Wilson with demolition charges; however, deliberations were brought to a halt by a report of a convoy leaving Argostoli to the north and likely to pass some sixty miles west of Navarin on the 14th. *Torbay* went off westwards, but nothing was seen and she was back at Methoni on the 15th. *Andrea Gritti* was given the *coup de grâce* with a torpedo; three sailing vessels were sunk in the Methoni Channel for the expenditure of thirty-one rounds of 4-inch ammunition.

On the night of the 16th Captain Wilson went to see what he could find in Navarin. He was away for four hours, and the round trip was almost twelve miles; all he got for his trouble was to be spotted and fired upon from Navarin town.

On the 17th the Italian Battle Fleet was reported at sea, and *Torbay* dashed off westwards to try to intercept. She was well on the way, doing mostly surface passage by day as well as by night, when a signal from Alexandria told her to do what she was already doing. There was no luck: the Battle Fleet passed some thirty miles to the west of *Torbay* during the 19th. There were other flies round the honeypot: the Malta-based U-class submarine *P 31* got in an attack.

Torbay was back at Navarin on the 20th. This time there was a destroyer, the *Vincenzo Gioberti*, at anchor in the harbour. Looking at Navarin harbour from the sea, you have, going from north-west to south-east, mainland, gap, Sphacteria island, gap, shoals and rocks, gap, Pylos island, the main entrance, the mainland. It seemed that it should be practicable to fire a torpedo between Sphacteria and Pylos and avoiding the rocks and shoals between. This was designed to give *Gioberti* trouble.

The attempt was duly made, with a torpedo set to run at eight feet depth. Miers, watching through the periscope, saw the torpedo's track curling away to starboard. Like a bird hypnotized by a snake, he watched, until we could hear the torpedo coming back at us. Then he ordered, 'Down periscope.' The torpedo whizzed past, at 40 knots, somewhere over the engine-room hatch. That gives an indication of how far *Torbay* had moved since firing the torpedo from the bow: about two thirds of her own length – say, 200 feet.

A torpedo carried its own engine, fuel and air to burn with the fuel. This system came into operation as soon as the torpedo left the submarine, and it soon reached the torpedo speed of 40 knots. Also becoming active as the torpedo was launched were its steering and depth-keeping mechanisms. The steering was by gyro compass which acted on a vertical rudder. The depth-keeping was by a hydrostatic mechanism which reacted to water pressure and acted on horizontal rudders. The steering and depth-keeping mechanisms were independent, yet they could interact. Should the vertical rudder be jammed or the gyro be haywire, so that the rudder was continuously over one way, the torpedo would assume a stern-down posture. This would cause it to rise above its set depth until the hydrostatics applied down rudder. The torpedo would then dip down, probably below its set depth, then rise again. Then the process would be repeated. Thus a torpedo which had gone berserk as regards its steering could be expected to 'porpoise' above and below its ordered depth.

After the torpedo had passed, to do at least two more circles, Miers ordered *Torbay* deep. His failure to give this order, as soon as there was evidence of circling, was a blunder of 'schoolboy howler' proportions. These are the parameters. *Torbay* was in theory good for 300 feet depth. In fact, post-war trials showed that she would not collapse until more like 600 feet. The Mark VIII++ torpedo, on the other hand, would have its innards crushed soon after eighty feet. Thus the best way to avoid was DOWN, DOWN, DOWN.

What about the first lieutenant? He could not see, but he could hear the Sonar operator's reports, as he listened to the torpedo; these showed clearly what was to happen. While Miers was mesmerized, Chapman should have ordered 'Flood Q' [the quick diving tank], group up [maximum motor power], full ahead together, 200 feet [or more]. Once embarked on this line of action, it would have been difficult for Miers to stop it; nor, awakened as from a trance, would he have wanted so to do. There is no doubt that Chapman should have pre-empted the Commanding Officer, just as he had in Loch Long almost a year earlier.

When you meet the guy who never makes mistakes, let me know.

Some two years later Chapman, now with his own command, *Upstart*, had a torpedo circle. This time there was no delay in the DOWN,DOWN,DOWN routine; all the more so since *Upstart*'s torpedo was fitted with a warhead actuated by magnetic influence. In *Torbay*'s case, the torpedo had a contact pistol, so that it had actually to hit something before it would explode. Even so, in *Torbay*'s case, if the torpedo had been a little too deep, it must have hit the engine-room; had *Torbay* been moving a fraction more slowly, it must have hit the conning tower or periscope standards. In either event, it is most unlikely that there would have been any survivors.

It was contemplated that Captain Wilson might go in at *Gioberti* that night, but the wind had got up and sea and swell conditions were unsuitable for a launch.

On the 22nd a schooner was demolished close to Navarin; it was as well that this was done smartly, because in the closing stages a shore battery opened fire.

By this time *Vincenzo Gioberti* had gone, but her place had been taken by another destroyer, the *Castore*; so it was decided to send in Wilson. It was calm, but it was also cold, and it was the latter, which defeated Wilson; he came back with his teeth chattering like castanets. Wet suits were in the future, and Wilson was a skinny little man; a plumper operator might have managed.

As described in *SBS in World War II*, Wilson was in due course to finish up as a prisoner of war, when he and his parent submarine failed to meet at the recovery rendezvous somewhere near Sicily. What exactly happened is not known; but it is the case that a submarine, if threatened by enemy surface patrols, would withdraw and would leave the folboteers to fend for themselves. This was a risk that these brave people took, and they knew it.

On the 23rd *Torbay* tried a torpedo through the Sphacteria rocks gap, as in the attempt on *Gioberti*. This time the torpedo behaved itself, and *Castore*'s bow section was a sad mess. The enemy responded by setting off a controlled minefield off Navarin entrance. But this was way off target; they must have judged the torpedo to have been fired from east of Pylos, whereas *Torbay* was, in fact, to the west of Pylos. Also, out came a motor anti-submarine boat; her ideas were more to the point, and she dropped five depth-charges, fairly close. The same day, before setting off back to Alexandria, *Torbay* tried another torpedo at a merchant ship near Navarin pier. The torpedo had to shave the rocks to the east of Sphacteria; but it did not; it exploded on them.

Christmas at sea was marked by a short service, and *Torbay* was back the day after Boxing Day.

One destroyer, one merchant ship, five sailing craft, two Special Operations launches; sixty-two air patrols, seventeen patrol vessels, five depth-charges.

Once again, on the approach to Alexandria, we had met a friendly force, of which we had not been warned, coming out.

11 The Lighter Side

Some episodes in the lives of submariners bent on having a Good Time

So far no mention has been made of what happened during rest periods between patrols. It should be remembered that many of Miers' people, and all his officers, were recently from school, with all the exuberance associated with schoolboy pranks. Nor was Miers himself above the occasional leg-pull – such as when he crept into his first lieutenant's cabin in the depot ship at dead of night and stole all his front and back studs. Then he got up early to see how the first lieutenant would manage blue uniform, with stiff collar and tie, for the 8 am ceremony of hoisting the White Ensign. The first lieutenant did manage, by begging, borrowing or stealing a set, which earned him a plus-point; moreover, he knew of nobody else around with such a sabotage-style sense of humour; so he challenged at breakfast and got the loot back.

This chapter is a small sample of what may be termed extra-curricular activities, when the young people, forced by the exigencies of war rather prematurely into positions of great responsibility, let down their hair. They were, after all, as 'ones born out of due time' and a bit like glasshouse strawberries, forced, to fruit early; so were many others – for example, Battle of Britain pilots.

On *Torbay*'s visit to Port Said for docking, the young gentlemen, to give them that compliment, lodged in an hotel called Café's Pension. Here, probably because of the ghost of Ferdinand de Lesseps, French rather than English was the norm; but Chapman and Campbell, who shared a double room, were that equal to the event that the Egyptian staff called them *'Les deux Français de numéro trente-neuf'*. From their vantage-point they observed a flat roof, which was the home of a Muscovy duck – in fact, almost certainly a drake. They determined to capture the bird, and they did, brought it back to the hotel room, made friends and fed it regularly.

A certain 'QZ' was also staying at Café's; he had an *amour*, and the pair were wont to sleep in the same room. However, one evening they went separate ways to different parties. When the lady returned, she was detained in the bar by one of the gang. In the meantime two others, with the help of a pass key, had obtained access to the tryst. Onto the pillow they put the over-fed duck, which promptly settled down to sleep. The miscreants then hid behind a floor-length arras and watched through chinks.

In came 'QZ', three parts cut, took off his jacket and patted the pillow. The Muscovy did not know this guy and bit his hand. 'QZ' seemed in no way perturbed and continued to disrobe. When the significance of this percolated the alcoholic minds of those behind the arras, it was more than they could bear. They collapsed to the deck in shakes of laughter, and their legs stuck out from under the arras. To whatever else 'QZ' had become accustomed, it did not include four-legged animals under the arras, and he sent the young people packing, and with contumely. But first they recovered their duck.

Before being returned to the owner, the bird emerged from its zip-up holdall, where it was happy to roost on other occasions; but the one described was surely its finest hour.

Day-old chicks are part of the stock-in-trade of Egyptian conjurors, known as 'Gulli Gulli men'. They can make chicks appear from such unlikely places as thin air and inside the fly buttons of a member of the audience. It is not so difficult as it sounds: the chicks are small enough to be enclosed in a hand, and there they are content, as they appreciate the warmth and the contact.

The young people got a friendly Gulli Gulli man to help. They practised with a half-pint tankard and were soon confident that they could make a chick appear from an empty chalice at the Christmas midnight service. The plot failed: *Torbay* was at sea returning from patrol at Christmas 1941; so the padre did not have a stroke after all.

Because of the danger of night air raids, no more than one submarine each side stayed alongside the depot ship at night. Any others had to shove off after tea, to dispersal berths or buoys.

All harbour movements were the first lieutenant's business, and he did or supervised them all until he was able to advise the captain that the third and fourth hands were competent to go solo. Thus it was that Campbell, on his own, took *Torbay* to a buoy one evening. Soon a person-to-person signal was delivered to Chapman: 'Please speak.' So he went to the signal deck, borrowed a night signalling lantern and chatted to Campbell in morse; submarines then had no radio telephone equipment. Campbell feared that he might have a berthing wire round the port shaft. One end had slipped overboard whilst he was under way. He had stopped the port motor, but it takes time for the shaft to stop; and the wire had been recovered minus an uncertain quantity off its end. That piece might be at the bottom of the harbour, or it might be wound round the shaft; if so, it could possibly mean going into dock.

Miers was warned, and Chapman suggested that he should go across at first light and dive, using Davis escape apparatus, to examine the shaft.

'No,' said Miers. 'If he thinks he may have done it, let him dive on it, but we will send Tono Kidd to go down with him.'

So it was done; in the early morning Miers and Chapman were on the promenade deck, eyes glued to binoculars. They were suddenly aware of a presence. The impressive figure of Captain Raw was behind them.

'Sir,' said Miers, 'I was going to send you a signal, but I do not yet know what to say; the third hand and the engineer are investigating.'

'So I saw,' said 'Sammy'. 'Let me know, when you know; and do not worry; I know which submarine Commanding Officers are training their young officers to take responsibility.'

In a few minutes Campbell and Tono climbed out of the water onto the stern. They held up four thumbs; the propeller must have made a clean cut.

We did not shave at sea, except to smarten up before return to harbour. There was the fresh water problem already described, and there was another reason. Suppose we were to be sunk, yet managed to survive as prisoners of war, then a hirsute bunch would arrive and be photographed at the first organized POW camp. At the first opportunity, if any, to escape, the last-minute preliminary would be to shave off; then the enemy would not have an up-to-date mug shot of the missing prisoner.

Miers' beard was looking rather good, gingery and full, so he decided to go into Alexandria with it still on. This caused a contretemps which he had not foreseen. The senior submarine officers were astonished that the usually meticulous and immaculate Miers should come in unshaven. They concluded that he must be over-tired and that he should be rested for a patrol, so that another would take *Torbay* out for her next trip.

This idea was anathema to Miers; he knew of many a submarine lost soon after replacing the Commanding Officer. He protested vigorously but was told to 'sit down in the boat' and do as he was told. But this he would not do; he exercised his right of appeal to the Commander-in-Chief, Sir Andrew Browne Cunningham. Little is known of what transpired, except that the flag lieutenant, before leaving the cabin whither he had ushered Miers, heard Sir Andrew's opening remark, 'I hear that you are being insubordinate.' Be that as it may, Miers took us on the next patrol, and nobody ever tried to rest him again.

On the day of his interview with Sir Andrew, Miers had been asked to lunch by the Consul-General, Clifford Heathcote-Smith. So had Kidd and Chapman, and they arrived on time, whereas Miers did not. Said Mrs Consul-General, after several rounds of cocktails, 'Well, I suppose we will just have to wait; the Commander-in-Chief does talk so much.' Sir Andrew was, in fact, known as a man of few words. He may have concluded that it was better to have Miers at sea rather than haranguing him in harbour.

Mary's House in Alexandria was a civilized house of pleasure. On the ground floor was a large lounge bar where, round the clock, you could take any drink you fancied; if not otherwise engaged upstairs, the girls were there. You were, of course, advised of the delights upstairs, but there was no element of compulsion; they were happy for you to drink with your friends downstairs. You might even meet Mary in the bar, but that would be a rare experience, for she was busy presiding over establishments in Alexandria, Cairo and Port Said.

One night in 1941 the Italians, no doubt by accident, managed to lob a bomb onto the roof of Mary's House in Alexandria. The bomb was of the semi-armour-piercing type intended for warships, so it ground its way through the roof and upper storeys and detonated in the lounge bar. Thus, apart from shrapnel and splinter wounds, the girls upstairs and their temporary partners got away with it. The lounge bar, on the other hand, was a charnel house of mangled heads, bodies and legs. There were no Torbays there that night, but there were a number of empty places at breakfast in the depot ship next morning. There has to be a moral; perhaps it could be, 'The Devil looks after his own.'

Mary rose to the occasion. The Alexandria girls were in a state of shock and not giving of their best, so she switched the Alexandria girls to Cairo, and the Cairo ones to a new place in Alexandria. Thus when *Torbay* got Cairo leave, about once every four months, we were with old friends who had much to tell us of their traumatic experiences.

*

When speaking about 'The Book', what is intended is not the Bible but *The King's* (now *Queen's*) *Regulations and Admiralty Instructions*. The Book is a massive tome and is supported by countless specialized manuals. But the basic Book, for the conduct of the Royal Navy, was, in short title, *KR & AI*. If in doubt, you could get there the answer, or at least a steer, provided you understood the index system.

Torbay was in harbour at Alexandria for New Year 1942. This period included the half-yearly promotions published on 31 December. It also included happenings not in 'The Book'.

Nothing is certain in an uncertain world, but there were strong indications that Miers would be promoted. There had been messages of warm congratulation from captain submarines and others. When *Torbay* returned from the patrol which had accounted for one U-boat and two ships by torpedo, and eight craft by gunfire, the battleship *Queen Elizabeth* had cleared lower deck, manned ship and cheered her into harbour. The *Queen Elizabeth* was the flagship of the Commander-in-Chief, Sir Andrew Cunningham, so her action must have been with his knowledge and approval. One would have been dim-witted indeed not to have discerned the indications.

One thing was clear. Were Miers to be promoted, his generous heart would impel him to throw a large party; and not in an hotel on shore, nor yet in the depot ship *Medway* but in his pride and joy, *Torbay*.

Being a year out of the builder's and doing arduous patrols, *Torbay*'s interior was getting to look grubby, as was accepted in wartime. However, the first lieutenant, as housekeeper, spoke with the people about it. Could we not paint out the torpedo stowage and accommodation areas, and the control room, so that Miers could throw a party in something looking brand new? This was a tall order during the festive season and in a period of supposed rest and recuperation. It was not in the Book. But the sailors did it, and some of their friends from depot ship and other submarines came to help. That is not in the Book, but that is the sort of people submariners are.

The promotion duly came, followed a few days later by a large lunch-time cocktail party for which the entire submarine was taken over. Miers' friends came from all over the fleet and from the shore. Sailors acted as waiters and were allowed also to serve themselves. That was not in the Book.

The interior décor of the submarine gave rise to such remarks as 'Unbelievable!', 'Like a peace-time inspection!' Commander 'Tubby' Linton, soon to be VC and later to be sunk by mines, in *Turbulent*, in the Bonifacio Strait, sought out the first lieutenant. 'It really is marvellous.'

Torbay had to slip from the depot ship at half past one, to allow another submarine to get alongside and under the crane. So the party dispersed back into HMS *Medway* soon after one o'clock. It was a day of brilliant winter sunshine, so many of the officers got a drink in the wardroom and took it out onto the promenade deck outside. The first lieutenant, preparing for the harbour movement, was aware that he had an unusually large and distinguished public gallery looking down from on high. Harbour movements were such a routine operation that, in those days, you did them with one officer and the duty watch, which would be one third or one quarter of the crew.

All was going according to plan until Able Seaman 'X', who had been a waiter and was one of the duty watch, appeared on the forward casing to handle securing wires. He was staggering. It seemed that he might at any time fall overboard. One can just imagine the malicious laughter: '*Torbay* threw a party, and then shoved off, shedding drunken sailors into the 'oggin' like autumn leaves.'

The Book says, 'Never approach, nor get into argument with, drunken or excited men.' This is a wise generalization, because, if it results that the man strikes a superior, that man is almost certainly for court martial. The Book would advise to get two of his kind, because he can hit them without its being a serious offence, plus a leading seaman or petty officer in charge, and have him frog-marched away, then to be charged with being drunk on duty. However, that would not look so good to the public gallery, nor would it reflect well on *Torbay*'s management.

These considerations flashed through the mind much

faster than it takes to read them. The first lieutenant climbed down from the bridge to the fore casing and spoke to Able Seaman X in a way that only he could hear:

'Thank you for coming up, X, but we can manage quite well without you. Why not go below and have a kip?'

'Oh, no, sir, I will be all right. It is my duty to be here.'

(Slowly, but incisively:) 'X, please, I want you to go below.'

X weaved his way below quietly, got his head down and slept peacefully until supper-time. He had given no trouble before, nor did he ever after. Indeed, after we returned to UK he got a commission in the Royal Naval Volunteer Reserve.

This incident was a bit like Stanley Holloway's 'Please, Sam, pick oop tha musket.' Perhaps thence came the idea, for X's first name was, in fact, Samuel. The happenings were in full view of the public gallery and attracted the same sort of comment as the submarine's décor. What was done was not in the Book, and of course it might not have worked. Even so, if you know each individual well, as in a small ship you can and should, you know at once what sort of approach is likely to be productive.

As the party dissolved, Tono Kidd down below was doing his best to ensure that nothing untoward occurred. It was only a short plank from *Torbay* to *Medway*'s long and steep accommodation ladder; even so, if Tono decided that an officer should not attempt the journey, he was laid out on a bunk or cushions in the fore part; sailors similarly found fallible were led to the after part.

All the same, X passed muster to report for duty on the casing. From the conversation it is clear that the only thing wrong with him was his legs; he was probably quite all right until hit by the fresh air. Chapman had seen this sort of thing happen at new season's scrumpy parties in Devonshire. So long as they were inside the warm, stuffy, smoky atmosphere of the farmhouse, the guests were all right; but the cool, night, autumn air went to the legs, so that they finished up collapsed in hedges and ditches. Then farmer Baker would get out the low loader, and he and Chapman would embark them, dump on doorstep, bang the knocker and go on to the next stop.

When the other submarine had got under the crane, *Torbay* came back outside her. There was still some clearing up after the party to be done. It was then that we noticed that our captured German and Italian ensigns were missing. They had been on display just below the forward hatch. It would not have been any of *Torbay*'s people, nor Miers' guests. Someone must have come aboard, in the hurly-burly of the party, and stuffed them up his jumper. This would probably be an already fat person. Miers and all *Torbay*'s crew were alerted as were *Medway*'s gangway staff in case someone tried to smuggle them ashore. Soon Miers asked the first lieutenant what else he was doing about it. The first lieutenant said that it was wise for Miers not to know too much at that stage. But he added, 'Sir, I think you will find that it will be all right.'

Later the second coxswain came to the first lieutenant. 'Sir, we know who, and we know where.'

'Excellent, well done. Take overwhelming numbers, and say, "Give over and that is the end of it, else we take you and your place apart." '

Around tea-time the second coxswain and the first lieutenant took the ensigns to Miers.

So *Torbay* ended a happy day. It was all the happier for the first lieutenant because he had not needed to charge anybody with anything. That always made for a happy day; but you won't find that in the Book.

Moving back a little, promotion day, 31 December 1941, was also New Year's Eve. This is, to the Scots, a major event known as Hogmanay. They, the Scots, are apt to go a bit screwball, and to eat haggis, and to drink scotch. *Torbay* was giving midnight leave at that time. You were supposed to come off in the midnight boat and not to slip back later by shoreboat felucca. The first lieutenant had his eye on the Scots that night. When the count was taken, two were missing, Miers and one able seaman.

On New Year's Day Miers enquired of the first lieutenant whether any Scots had over-stayed their leave.

'In fact, sir, only two, you and Able Seaman Y, the trainer

of the gun.'

'I did not know that you knew about me. But, in the circumstances, you cannot put Y in my report.'

'So I had guessed. I have dismissed the charge.'

'And?'

'Oh, he is painting out the auxiliary machinery space in his spare time.'

Nor was that in the Book.

The auxiliary machinery space was a deck down, but it was just below the ladder from the forward hatch. Thus the guests coming down on Miers' day did not go down there, but they could not fail to see it, glistening white and not a dingy dungeon. The first lieutenant had found time in the dog watches to visit to see how Y was getting on, and to wield an extra paintbrush. At length the fiddly labour of Hercules was complete.

Said Y, 'I reckon you got a bloody good deal out of this.'

'Yes, indeed, but perhaps we both did; you have a clean conduct sheet; and your half-yearly report, which I have just written, commends you for application and diligence.'

> Now these are the laws of the Navy,
> Unwritten and varied they be;
> And he that is wise will observe them,
> Going down in his ship to the sea.
> As the wave rises clear to the hawse pipe,
> Washes aft and is lost in the wake,
> So shall ye drop astern, all unheeded,
> Such time as the law ye forsake.
>
> (Final verse of 'The Laws Of The Navy')

> If at your risk you choose to ignore them,
> Be very sure that you know what you do.
> If your action results in some mayhem,
> Nobody will plead excuses for you.
>
> (Additional verse, 1988)

Able Seaman Phillips was a Reservist; that is to say that he had done twelve years Royal Navy service and had then been put to the Royal Fleet Reserve. When the latter was mobilized, Phillips was recalled to the colours.

Phillips had been a gunlayer, but he had not requalified

during the prescribed period, so he was re-engaged in his earlier role of able seaman torpedoman. When *Torbay* had had to sail from the Holy Loch at short notice, the gunlayer was one of those on leave, and there was no spare available. But Miers knew that Phillips had been a gunlayer, so that was that; Phillips became gunlayer and captain of the gun. As such he was in every way outstanding; but for him cash was no problem, and he simply did not want the extra responsibilities of being a leading seaman. Even so, he was persuaded that it was his patriotic duty to sit the Board for Candidates for Leading Seaman. The first lieutenant was a member of the board; he watched in dismay as Phillips stood speechless and flummoxed when asked to give instructions for a simple evolution.

That evening Phillips sought out the first lieutenant in his cabin. 'Sorry if I let you down at the power of command session this morning, sir. My wits just seemed to desert me.'

'Even so, thank you, Phillips.'

Some time later Phillips was told to stand fast from the eight o'clock muster and to report to the first lieutenant in his cabin.

'Oh yes, Phillips; you are to get into your best long white suit; the Commander-in-Chief, Sir Andrew Cunningham, wants to see you at eleven o'clock.'

'Who, me?'

'Yes, you. Carry on, Phillips; oh, Phillips:'

'Sir.'

'I think that we may – but, of course, I say this politely – I think that we may have you foxed.'

At eleven the Commander-in-Chief, by virtue of his powers to make special advancement, created Phillips leading seaman for outstanding leadership and gallantry in charge of *Torbay*'s gun.

That evening Phillips found the first lieutenant in his cabin. 'Thank you, sir, for everything; you will understand that I say this politely; I have promised myself, some day, some time, to get back at you.'

'Well then, see to it, Phillips; you are that daft, it will take you all your time; of course, I say this politely.'

Even so, Phillips scored his goal in Chapter 15.

There was not much drinking at sea on patrol; a glass of sherry after tea and a can of beer with supper was about it, except for massaging an aching tooth with whisky; but there was quite a lot of drinking in harbour.

In submarines the engineer officer, if you had one, was the wine caterer, whereas in big ships it would be the young doctor. Thus in *Torbay* Tono Kidd was wine caterer. To make accounting more simple, we preferred to start each harbour period with a stock of whole bottles. Therefore, during the quiet dived day before the night approach to Alexandria, after breakfast Tono and the first lieutenant mustered the wines and spirits. Anything that was opened they consumed, but they were still bright-eyed and bushy-tailed for entering harbour next morning. It is astonishing what a young physique can tolerate, but they would not have passed the breathalyser.

This was called 'the levelling operation.'

A well-run and favourite haunt of the sailors ashore was the Alexandria Fleet Club. One night some of the chief petty officers and petty officers invited David Campbell to visit them. A peculiarity of Campbell was that he usually took with him a Colt 0.45 calibre revolver when he went ashore; he was quite adept with the pistol, else he might not have survived the treachery described in Chapter 6.

Late on in the evening it seemed to Campbell that it would add to the gaiety of nations to shoot out the lights; so he did. But the club officials were offended, and a deputation called next day on Miers to complain and to suggest that the erring young man should be disciplined. Miers pointed out that Campbell was a guest, not a member; therefore, as in most club rules, the hosts were responsible for the behaviour of their guest. The deputation retired; they had not thought of things in quite that way.

What Miers said to Campbell is uncertain, but it was some time before Campbell next went ashore; nor was he to be seen drinking in HMS *Medway*'s wardroom ante-room; if he wanted a drink, he had to go down the boat to get it.

That was Miers all over. He could be strict but he would deal with his people, and nobody, but nobody else, would be allowed to touch them.

Here is another example. Miers and Chapman were ashore in the same bar. Chapman, who was born Archbishop of Tease, got under the skin of an elderly, retired but re-employed lieutenant-commander; this one in due course asked Chapman for his name and ship, obviously with a view to making a formal complaint.

Said Chapman, 'It seems that I have offended. I am sorry. I did not mean to. However, my commanding officer is over there; you could speak with him now if you wish.'

Miers explained that there might be an excess of exuberance in that we were celebrating his DSO and Chapman's DSC. He of offended dignity agreed to let the matter drop. That was that, except that, on the way home, Miers tore Chapman up for arse paper.

The subject of the teasing was that the elder in question was ashore in the evening in khaki battledress with naval insignia. He should not have been; the Commander-in-Chief's Mediterranean Fleet Orders were quite clear on this sort of point; Sir Andrew was a stickler for correct dress come what may, and the officer should have been in blue uniform like the rest of us. Sir Andrew would not even let his submariners wear khaki shorts and shirts in harbour, though this had been the norm in China whence had come the 'O'-, 'P'- and 'R'-class submarines of the First Flotilla. It could be that the elder was wise not to press the issue; it might even have bounced.

It was quite normal for the watch-keeping officers to be 'one in three' – that is, two hours on and four hours off. But the four hours off included such things as meals, closing up at diving stations to dive or to surface, and any other action that might be triggered by the approach of an enemy. The engineer officer helped out by keeping some dived watches, and of course a 'fifth hand' if embarked also took his turn. Even so, shortage of sleep was the norm, and when you did manage to 'get your head down', it was to a deep sleep of exhaustion.

A favourite trick with a newly joined officer was to send the control-room messenger to shake him at ten minutes to his watch, with the message, 'It is cold and wet on the bridge.' Our tyro would climb laboriously into woollens, then waterproof trousers and jacket, then mittens. Then he would sling his binoculars round his neck, stumble still half asleep into the control room and make his way to the ladder leading up the conning tower. At about this point the ribald laughter of the control room crew would properly awaken him to the fact that he had been called for a dived watch, with no cold or wet.

'Z' was a mature, important and much-respected person, but something had gone wrong, so that Miers had awarded seven days stoppage of leave. The day before sailing for patrol, 'Z' put in a request to see the first lieutenant on a personal matter; so the coxswain brought him along.

'Would you like the coxswain to leave us?'

'Oh no, I am quite happy for the coxswain to stay.'

'Right, then what is the problem?'

'It is this, sir. I am under stoppage of leave, as you know, and this is my last day of stoppage. But we sail tomorrow tea-time, and my Little Girl will be heartbroken if I do not visit before we sail. Is there anything you can do?'

(Oh, oh, heartbroken? With the whole of the rest of the Mediterranean Fleet to console her? I know who will be heartbroken!)

'Your punishment was awarded by the captain; I may not annul it. But, if you agree, I am prepared to suspend it for seven days; by that time we should be off either Taranto or Benghazi, and you may not wish to go ashore there, not yet anyway. What say?'

'Thank you, sir.'

'Give him his liberty card, coxswain; and "Z", this had better be between us three.'

Oh well, better to take to sea a contented man than one frustrated.

The captain's steward was a Cockney hostilities-only rating called Eddie Gardner; he had been in the butchering trade. When he volunteered, he asked for a job in the open air. But, in the exigencies of war, needs have to be balanced against preferences; so Gardner was assigned as steward, whose duties are obviously mainly between decks. Then he volunteered for submarines and did the submarine training class.

Meanwhile *Torbay* was being built at Chatham, and Miers and his officers rented a house in Prospect Row. The submarine was not yet habitable – not that you lived in submarines in harbour except if there was no alternative, and accommodation in the Royal Naval Barracks did not appeal. Then *Torbay* was warned to expect, and to entertain, an important visitor from the United States Navy; the officer wished to inspect a British submarine under construction. Miers decided that they must all have dinner in what they called 'Torbay House' in Prospect Row. Already a cook had joined *Torbay* and could cook the dinner; but so far no steward had joined to serve it; thus Miers got on to the authorities responsible, asking them to put the skids under a steward for *Torbay*. So Gardner got the bum's rush; he arrived, breathless, during the afternoon of the day of the dinner.

'Thank God you've arrived. We have a dinner party tonight,' said Miers.

'Thank God I have,' said Gardner. 'I found *Torbay* all right, but I thought I would never find Prospect Row.'

'Well, you have; what training have you had?'

'I have just done the submarine training class.'

'Yes, of course, but as a steward I mean.'

'A fortnight's disciplinary course and three weeks arms drill.'

'Disciplinary course' may sound like a form of punishment, but it was not that at all. It was to teach a new recruit the essentials of behaviour; how to dress, how to sling and use a hammock, to stand, to march, to salute, when to have cap on, when cap off, and so on; and never to seek your master in the wardroom ante-room if wearing an overall, because that costs your master drinks all round for all the other officers present. So at least Gardner was not wet behind the ears in these respects; but, as regards serving at table, that had to be a crash course by Miers after tea. No wonder Gardner spilt the soup all over the American.

But that was just one of these difficult starts; Gardner was very bright and quick on the uptake. In Chapter 13 he is recorded as the sightsetter of the gun; this was a task he performed in more than twenty actions, and he did it very well, and for it he was 'mentioned in despatches for distinguished service'. Gardner also loved joining in to make one in such jobs as painting the outside of the submarine; after all, these jobs were in the open air.

12 Mediterranean Submarines and the Wider Scene

Torbay's small place in world-war strategy

It was about Christmas 1941 that the First Submarine Flotilla decided to make the montage of Jolly Rogers as illustrated. This, be it remembered, is a 'snapshot', taken at a moment in time and probably already out of date when printed, because there were always some of the flotilla out at sea and doing, and we might not know what until they came back to harbour. In the snapshot, *Torbay* had been in the Mediterranean business for some eight months, *Triumph* even longer, whereas *Thorn* had but recently arrived.

Torbay was not fighting a one-man submarine war, nor was the First Flotilla. At Malta was the Tenth Flotilla, strategically placed across the main Axis supply route to North Africa. They were bombed out in early 1942, but as soon as conditions in Malta eased, they were back again. At the beginning of 1944 they moved to La Maddalena, in the Bonifacio Strait between Corsica and Sardinia. This was because their final operational area was from Port Vendres, by the Franco-Spanish frontier, to Genoa in north-east Italy.

At Gibraltar was the Eighth Flotilla. Later, when Algiers was in Allied hands, they moved thither, so as to be closer to the action which became primarily central Mediterranean.

The First Flotilla moved to Beirut in the Lebanon in

1942, when Rommel was only about sixty miles from Alexandria. In 1944 they moved to Malta and absorbed some of the Tenth Flotilla from La Maddalena. This was because the Allied 'Anvil' landings had taken place in the South of France, so there were no longer any enemies for the Tenth between Port Vendres and Genoa. Thus it was that the writer did his first Mediterranean war patrol, under First Flotilla auspices, in April 1941 and his last, again under First Flotilla auspices, in the Aegean in October 1944.

The Allied submarines (Polish, Dutch, Greek, Free French and then Giraud French took part) did not have it all their own way. Of those shown in the First Flotilla montage, the following were lost within a year or so: *Talisman, Triumph, Parthian, Thunderbolt, Tetrarch, Perseus, Thorn*.

At an earlier stage, soon after Italy entered the war in mid 1940, First Flotilla losses were particularly savage. It was sometimes a case of sending three boats out and getting one back. The flotilla had arrived from China, with large, ocean-going, old, noisy submarines. These were not best suited to the Mediterranean war; nor were the intelligence and briefing supplied all that good; nor was the state of training and awareness all that it should have been. Lessons hard learnt in the North Sea had not been absorbed. For this last point 'Head Office' must take some blame. The writer, first going to war in a submarine on anti-invasion patrols in the North Sea in August 1940, was interested to read the two or three sheets of advice on how to conduct one's boat in war. The piece was called 'Submarine Principles' and had been written by Commander Studholme in 1917.

It was not until newer, more suitable submarines of the 'S', 'T' and 'U' classes arrived that Mediterranean submarines started to show a real profit in relation to the lives and material expended.

To quote the reckoning from an HM Stationery Office publication,* at the time of the surrender of the Italian Fleet

---

* *His Majesty's Submarines* (HMSO, 1945, prepared for the Admiralty by the Ministry of Information).

in 1943, the following was the position in relation to submarines and sinkings: '1,335,000 tons of Axis shipping were on the bottom; and 41 of their number lay there too.'

Three of the 1941-2 submarine commanding officers were awarded the Victoria Cross. In this order they were, Wanklyn of *Upholder* (Tenth Flotilla), Miers of *Torbay* (First Flotilla) and Linton of *Turbulent* (First Flotilla). Only *Torbay* survived her Mediterranean tour. *Upholder* fell to Italian depth-charges, and *Turbulent* to Italian mines.

As a tribute to the past, all three names feature in the 1988 Submarine Fleet.

In Chapter 10 we had reached the turn of the year 1941-2; that is a good time for taking stock. What was different at the end of *Torbay*'s first year in commission, and in what way did it affect her?

As said in Chapter 1, in June the Soviet Union and in December the United States had become ranged against the Axis Powers. In the general picture, that made all the difference in the world. As Churchill has said, 'We should not be wiped out. Our history would not come to an end. We might not even have to die as individuals.' Churchill did go on to say, 'I expected terrible forefeits in the East.'*

He got these all right as, one by one, places fell to the Japanese onslaught: Hong Kong, the Philippines, Malaya, Singapore, the Dutch East Indies, Burma. It was not until the American naval victories of the Coral Sea and Midway Island, in May and June 1942, that the Japanese tide was stemmed. All this meant that the enemy seemed to be getting ever closer to the back door of the Middle East, and ever closer to the position where he could interdict, or even sever, our supply route round the Cape of Good Hope. For these reasons we invaded Madagascar and put what reinforcements we could find, particularly fighter aircraft, into Ceylon.

It also meant that such a thing as an Eastern Mediterranean battle fleet was a thing of the past; any

* See Churchill, House of Commons in secret session 23/4/42, cited in *Sea Devils* by Commander Prince Valerio Borghese (Arrow Books, 1956).

units like that, when and if available, would be needed further east. Already there was no Mediterranean battle fleet; the two battleships which had been able to remain on station after the Battle of Crete, the *Queen Elizabeth* and the *Valiant*, had just been 'done' by Italian human torpedoes in Alexandria harbour. Though apparently still there, and in business, they were sitting on the bottom, but with false water lines painted on to disguise the fact. Even so, by early January the Italians knew that a substantial success had been achieved and that their battle fleet had no British counterpart.

That left light cruisers, destroyers and escort vessels. In relation to the Italian fleet, these were defensive forces. There was no way, particularly without air support, that they could carry the war to the enemy; only submarines and aircraft could do that. At least the submarines did; there was no question of an 'iron ring' round Alexandria and Port Said, in case the Axis tried to invade Egypt by sea. Egypt was reinforced by torpedo aircraft from home, but this was defensive, and the Royal Air Force were on the point of being bombed out of their advanced base in Malta.

When heavy forces were required, such as to break the blockade of Malta in 'Operation Pedestal' in August 1942, they had to be found from forces normally in the Atlantic. Thus Pedestal had two battleships, four aircraft-carriers, seven cruisers and thirty-two destroyers. The operation succeeded, but there were heavy losses, and less than half the convoy of fourteen merchant ships got through. Still, that was enough to put Malta back into business, particularly as a base for aircraft and submarines; and Alamein was soon to turn the tide, on land, in North Africa.

However, at the turn of the year 1942, and for half or more of it, the favourable developments just described were still in the crystal ball; hopes perhaps, facts no. Malta was about to become untenable by submarines and aircraft; her surface force of cruisers and destroyers had, some time since, been wiped out on Italian minefields. It all added up to the onus falling ever more on the

Alexandria submarines. Thus, although there was pressure to send some through the canal to help out in the Far East, only a couple did go through in early 1942. The submarines simply could not be spared from what they were doing, and from where they were doing it; as Admiral Cunningham said, to him his submarines were worth their weight in gold. What would have been the use of keeping the back door open, if that had meant the enemy's coming in through the front door?

To add to the possibilities of doom and gloom was the question of what would happen to the Soviet Union. Hitler's diversion, to Yugoslavia and Greece, had delayed his attack on the USSR by several weeks of good campaigning weather. Thus the Russians were saved as much by winter as by their own efforts. Through ignoring what had seemed obvious to British Intelligence – that is, the evidence that they were about to be attacked – they had lost half their Air Force on the ground right at the start; and whole armies were rounded up and carted off to slave labour and death. Their Navy was a non-event and so remained for the duration. Furthermore, they had shown themselves to be markedly incompetent in their war with Finland in 1939, and there was so far no evidence to show that they had got any better.

There was a strong and well-informed school of thought, in the United Kingdom, which held that the Soviet Union would not survive the German spring and summer onslaught of 1942 but would collapse and opt out, as in 1917.

So, if *Torbay*, in her few months remaining on station, should seem to take unusual risks, the motivation should be clear. The best way we could help the cause was to follow a dictum of Napoleon, *'L'attaque, toujours l'attaque.'*

8th and 9th Patrols 1941/42

8th Patrol 9th to 27th December 1941

9th Patrol 8th to 31st January 1942

400

200

0

Miles

N

TURKEY

BEIRUT

CYPRUS

PORT SAID

ALEXANDRIA

EGYPT

LANDING 13/1

SCHOONER 12/12

Crete

GREECE

ATHENS

Peloponnese

TOBRUK

DERNA

Cyrenaica

BENGHAZI

MV 15/12
3 CAIQUES 15/12

SCHOONER 22/12

DESTROYER 23/12

MEDITERRANEAN SEA

CRUISERS
MISSED 22/1

TARANTO

ITALY

MESSINA

SICILY

MALTA

TRIPOLI

LIBYA

13 Ninth Patrol –
Crete, Gulf of Taranto

A Special Operation successfully completed – and an operation that never happened

This patrol was from 8th to 31 January 1942. It was noted for the voyage of the *Mauretania* and for a medical problem.

The so-called *Mauretania* was, for those days, a really jumbo-sized rubber boat, ten feet long by five wide. A party of Germans had used it to land, close west of Alexandria, from a U-boat; the Germans were apprehended and their splendid toy was confiscated. The boat was lent to *Torbay* for the purpose of landing bulky stores for our friends in Crete; these stores included an electric generator driven by a windmill.

The chosen landing-point was Triaklisia in south-eastern Crete, and the 10th and 11th were spent in periscope reconnaissance of this and an alternative beach. A south-westerly (that is, onshore) gale was blowing. Conditions were not much better on the 12th, when the first attempt was made. Our embarked party included two officers, one non-commissioned officer and four Greeks; this party had two folbots. One folbot was sent inshore to establish contact; it succeeded but was damaged beyond repair in the surf. Two officers, however got safely ashore in a small rubber boat, helped by the following wind. *Torbay* tried to launch the second folbot, but it was damaged beyond repair in the attempt; that was the only time this ever happened. That left the *Mauretania*; it was spread out, and whilst some pumped with several pairs of bellows, others started loading stores. Of a sudden, *Mauretania* started to deflate; the sails of the windmill had made a large gash in its buoyancy part. That was that for the night. The first lieutenant thought ruefully that it had not been the best advertisement for the doyen of Special Operations; and this in spite of the fact that we had just been cheered by the news that the Commander-in-Chief had specially advanced Leading Seaman Armishaw to petty officer for outstanding service. Armishaw was the second coxswain, and the first lieutenant's right-hand man in the Special Operations casing party.

Augustus William Illesley Armishaw was a quiet but most competent man – almost, one might say, a 'born' leader. Like Phillips, he was a mature man mobilized from the Royal Fleet Reserve. He came to *Torbay* on 22 March 1941, as one of the replacements for those on leave; he was an able seaman, with a DSM gained in North Sea patrols; he got a bar to this in *Torbay*. By about mid 1941 he was leading seaman and second coxswain, which is a petty officer's billet; now, six months later, he was a petty officer. After his *Torbay* days he became acting chief petty officer and came in late 1942 as coxswain of *H 33*, and then on to *Upstart*, when Chapman commanded those submarines. Alas, after a few months in *Upstart*, his health failed and he had to withdraw.

On 13 January *Torbay* went deep and raised both periscopes. It was then possible to spread out and fully to examine the *Mauretania* in the control room. There was only the one big gash, but a thing we did not have was a suitable puncture-repair outfit. The chief engine-room artificer, Herbert Pinch, had a look; he proposed padded steel plates within and without and bolted together. He went off, made them and fitted them, and *Mauretania* was back in business.

On the 13th was the second and successful main landing attempt. *Mauretania* was inflated and loaded; the weather had eased but, even so, the idea of loading the boat bobbing about by the forward hydroplanes did not appeal. *Mauretania* was loaded on the casing, just abaft the forward hatch so that the transit of stores was simple. Then her crew boarded; that was Tono Kidd, Stoker Patrick Conaty, Lieutenant Edwin Gage (embarked for experience), one seaman and four Greeks. Here one may remark that there were not demarcation disputes in *Torbay* or other submarines; stokers would be in the gun's crew, and in *Torbay* Eddie Gardner, the captain's steward, was the sightsetter.

When all was ready and the fore hatch shut, the first lieutenant advised Miers. He then dived the submarine. As the water came over the casing, the first lieutenant's party pushed *Mauretania* clear; they were then to swim about or cling to the jumping wire, until *Torbay* came up again. In the event, the *Mauretania* floated off easily and the casing party were never much more than up to their waists in January water. As Tono and party paddled away, they kept silence; but the first lieutenant, in his heart, was singing, 'Ah Ye Oh Koh, so all for each, until we reach, the journey's end' (*Sanders of the River*, Paul Robeson).

The *Mauretania* unloaded on the beach and came back with the stranded folboteers and one Austrian deserter. The latter had no English, but one of our able seaman had good German; with his help, the first lieutenant carried out a friendly interrogation at intervals over the next few days and compiled an intelligence report. The product was low-level intelligence, as would be expected from a private soldier, but it did include political, military and local Cretan elements.

Miers commented: '... the success of the operation was mainly because of the skill and endurance of the personnel concerned, who, under the orders of the First Lieutenant, seem to be quite undaunted however unpleasant the conditions may be.'

Torbay was then involved in attempts to intercept the Italian battle fleet. She was ordered to proceed with despatch to the Gulf of Taranto and to come under the orders of the Malta submarine command. Surface passage was made by day as well as by night until diving at 1100

on the 15th, when Italy was very close. *Torbay* was in her
ordered position by midnight, and the line up in the Gulf
was: to our north, the Polish submarine *Sokol*; to our south,
Una,* *Upholder* and *Thrasher*. *Torbay* communicated by
supersonic underwater telegraphy with her neighbours to
north and south.

In the next few days a small patrol vessel and three
destroyers were seen; they were left alone, for we were
after bigger game. On the 19th *Torbay* was recalled, but
Miers did not agree; *Torbay* moved north to the position
which we knew *Sokol* had vacated, and spent the 20th
between fifteen and twenty miles south of Taranto itself.
That night Miers asked for an extension on patrol, and this
was granted.

About three in the morning of the 22nd what turned out
to be a destroyer was sighted only about a mile away;
visibility was very poor, in mist; *Torbay* dived and was not
detected. This patrolling destroyer was an indication, and
sure enough, at about 1400 three cruisers and six
destroyers were seen dashing south-eastwards at 20
knots. Six torpedoes were fired at a range estimated at
8,000 yards, but it was probably more. Range estimation
relied on knowing something like the enemy's masthead
height or funnel height; a slight discrepancy here will lead
to a considerable error at long ranges. There was no result,
which was disappointing, as this was *Torbay*'s first and
only chance at large enemy warships. Once again, all we
could do was to make an enemy report in the hope that
someone else could get them. It took *Torbay* forty-five
minutes to clear the report, and during this period she did
three crash dives because of patrolling aircraft.

Here one may mention some peculiarities of the
high-frequency radio which submarines used for trans-
missions. Submarine transmitters, for space reasons, were
relatively low-powered, so that the signal would be
relatively weak. But submarines used special callsigns,
and at radio stations throughout the world these were

---

* Pat Norman, to be *Torbay*'s commanding officer in the third
commission.

known. Anyone hearing one of these callsigns would know that it was a submarine, sticking its neck out by transmitting at all, and risking being pinpointed by radio direction-finding. The submarine at once got the Austin Reed service (preferential treatment).

It was also the case, because of a phenomenon known as 'skip distance', that the listening station closest might be in the 'skip' and quite unable to hear. For example, several times in the Mediterranean the writer had hoped to raise Malta, but it might be Vancouver or New South Wales who would answer, 'I hear you. Send your message.'

It was soon after leaving Crete that the coxswain reported that he had put Stoker George sick with a sore throat. (George was his surname; we did not use Christian names between officers and ratings, except perhaps in off-duty moments in pubs.) George was turned in a bunk in the after ends of the submarine; there lived all the engine-room department except the engine-room artificers and the engineer officer.

In those far-off days, the first lieutenant, assisted by the coxswain, was supposed to be the boat's medical officer. Consequently Chapman went to have a look at George from time to time. George got steadily worse, throatwise, until he could swallow only fluids; Miers was alerted and went to see for himself. By this time George was in considerable discomfort and had difficulty in breathing.

Miers had a problem. In later days, one might have asked a Catalina (PBY) flying boat to land close by and do a Casualty evacuation (Casevac) to Egypt. But, Middle East Air Forces did not have any Catalinas; they were fighting the Battle of the Atlantic against the U-boats. In any case, with the overwhelming enemy air superiority in the Mediterranean at the time, it was debatable whether a Catalina could have reached us; equally it was rather unlikely that the transfer could be done without interruption, possibly fatal to both aircraft and submarine.

Miers asked the first lieutenant to speak to him in his cabin. Could it be diphtheria? If so, the whole of the engine-room department, and via them the rest of us, were at risk. Then he would have no alternative but to abandon patrol and make haste to Alexandria.

'Sir,' said the first lieutenant, 'it is not diphtheria, else I would have smelt it, just as I did in the case of my wife. What he has got is some sort of glandular infection; we are giving him M&B, but so far it seems not to do him any good.'

'But, if he cannot breathe, he is going to die; so what are you going to do?'

'Well, you realize that the coxswain has done a first aid course, but, owing to the pressure of events, I have not done even that. However, I have read that you cut open the throat and fish about until you find the windpipe, which is a whitish-looking tube. Then you make an incision and insert a pipette or even a straw, sometimes called a tracheotomy tube; then the lungs can bypass the nose and throat. Even so, how you stop the bleeding I do not know; but the coxswain knows how to sew up a wound.'

'Well then,' said Miers 'obviously, you know about it. We will give George another twenty-four hours to get better; if not, you will operate, and I will help you!'

'But, sir,' said the first lieutenant, 'I might so easily kill him.'

'Even so, I am not going to abandon patrol for the sake of one stoker. If I did, he could well die before we get back; if he cannot breathe, he is going to die anyway.'

On his next visit, Miers told Stoker George what lay ahead. This seemed to reassure rather than to frighten, and he soon began to mend. But for the next day, for the only time in the commission, the first lieutenant had genuine fear. Sleep was elusive; the constant thought – in fact, prayer – was. '*Domine, non sum dignus*. [Lord, I am not worthy.] Please take this one away from me.'

Twenty-four hours later, Stoker George was vastly better; he resumed full duty before we returned to Alexandria.

It is interesting to consider the interactions here. Stoker George's condition was alarming, above all to him;

consequently there was anxiety, particularly in him. Then Miers told him that his officers would operate. The stoker had faith in his officers; they had not failed before, so all would be well. Thus the anxiety departed from him; but it rushed into the first lieutenant, just as the evil spirit, cast out by Christ, rushed into the Gadarene swine. We will never know whether it was relief of tension or M&B which did the trick, but it may have been some of each.

Nearly half a century later Chapman spoke about the problem to a surgeon, remarking that the only time we really needed a doctor we did not have one, though we had had Surgeon Lieutenant Jones some patrols before.

Said the surgeon, 'How would you have opened the throat?'

'With a wide slit across, so as to get fingers in to find the windpipe.'

'That is right; how could you know?'

'I did not.'

One Special Operation, a disappointment, a near miss from probable mayhem, twenty-seven air patrols, thirteen patrol vessels.

14   Tenth Patrol –
Cephalonia, Gulf of Patras, Corfu, Gulf of Taranto, Messina, Benghazi, Apollonia

'A calculated act of most conspicuous bravery' –
Torbay's *Corfu operation*

This patrol was from 20 February to 18 March.

Whilst on the way to Cephalonia, *Torbay* received enemy reports indicating that the Gulf of Taranto might be a good place to be. But this was about three days passage away, and the weather was very bad, so Miers decided to follow existing instructions.

The weather was still adverse, with wind, rain and low visibility when *Torbay* was alerted to the probable approach of a tanker and a destroyer. These were seen at 0200 on the 27th. At that time *Torbay* was almost ahead of the tanker; so *Torbay* dived, opened the range and surfaced to attack from the quarter. One torpedo was fired, from close range on a very broad track. It did not hit; the sea was coming from astern of *Torbay*, and the consequent yawing probably meant that the torpedo was off course. The destroyer then saw *Torbay* and turned towards her at a range of about half a mile.

Miers ordered to dive but found to his dismay that he could not shut the upper conning tower hatch (upper lid). After several attempts he roared, 'Stand by lower lid' (lower conning tower hatch); then down he came, quick as down a greasy pole, and the lower lid was slammed shut. Meanwhile the submarine was diving, and the first lieutenant already had the ballast pump going full bore, pumping water out of 'O' tank, the midships auxiliary ballast tank. This was because he knew that a flooded conning tower would hold some five tons of extra and unwanted water.

The extra water was not the only problem. The conning tower had various electrical circuits; these were splash-tight but not pressure-tight. To remind us of this, as *Torbay* was passing forty feet, the klaxon horns started a continuous blare; the circuit had shorted. The first lieutenant glanced at the electrical artificer, Edwin Rintoul; a look of intense concentration passed over his face; then he reached up to the deckhead and pulled out the right fuse in a matter of perhaps five seconds. The destroyer dropped eleven depth-charges, but none was close enough to cause worry. The electrical circuits in the conning tower, however, suffered damage which could be repaired only in harbour, and this was a handicap for the rest of the patrol.

When all was quiet, *Torbay* surfaced, with Miers going up through the gun tower hatch. The conning tower was drained down into the bilges, and then the lower lid was opened. Miers meanwhile was seeing what had gone wrong with the upper lid. What he found made him eat humble pie. The pillow, which he used when resting on the bridge chart table at night on the surface, had floated to the top of the upper lid counter-weight during *Torbay*'s first dive. At the second dive it was stopping the movement of the counter-weight and jamming the hatch half open. Miers had been accusing Tono Kidd in particular, and the engine-room department in general, of not doing their maintenance work properly. These unworthy aspersions were withdrawn with a handsome apology.

In the afternoon of the same day a coastal steamer was sunk by gunfire; there was another coaster, and an anti-submarine trawler; but shore batteries took exception and, after they had landed shell within fifty yards of

Torbay, Miers decided to call it off. Two flying boats patrolled the area until sunset, and next day, the 28th, much patrolling and mine-sweeping was observed at the scene of the crime.

On 1 March off Cape Dukato in Levkas, a destroyer detected *Torbay* and hunted for an hour, dropping seven depth-charges; but these did no damage. This could not be said of the events of 3 March. Miers sought to attack a Cortatone-class destroyer in the late afternoon of that day. She either saw the periscope or got Sonar contact, for in she came with a pattern of six depth-charges. These were very close; *Torbay* was lifted bodily five feet, and there was significant, but controllable, damage throughout the boat. Depth-gauges, ammeters, compass, mechanical indicators and so on were broken or reading bogus values. The only human injury was when the ten-inch signal projector, stowed in a bracket behind the galley, jumped out of its perch and cut the cook's head. The destroyer dropped twelve more depth-charges, but these were nothing like so close as her first shot, which had given us a severe shaking.

The most tiresome part of the damage related to compasses. The helmsman had, in front of him, a repeater from the gyro compass; but that was no good, for the gyro was precessing – that is, going slowly round and round with its alarm bell jangling – until Rintoul switched off the alarm circuit. The helmsman also had, in front but to his left, an illuminated card from the main magnetic compass. This was on the bridge, but an optical tube of prisms and mirrors conveyed an image to the control room. But this was no good either, as some moisture had got into the tube, and all the helmsman could see was mist.

So down from its stowage above the helmsman came a small, portable magnetic compass, known with good reason as 'Faithful Freddie'. Freddie had had such a jolting as almost certainly to be inaccurate; but at least it was steady on something, and that was a lot better than nothing.

Tono Kidd rigged heaters to dry out the magnetic compass tube, whilst Campbell and Rintoul attended to the gyro. In due course both the main compasses were back in business, and Faithful Freddie retired to his shelf. He deserved a medal.

It seems clear, from what happened, that the first and damaging pattern of depth-charges had been set to explode too deep. *Torbay* was at about eighty feet and would hardly have had time to go any deeper; but she would not have done so anyway. The only times the writer remembers going below one hundred feet was during deep diving trials and to get away from some tiresome patrol craft, as described in the next chapter. Miers preferred to stay relatively shallow, even when under attack, for a number of reasons. A return to periscope depth, to look at the situation, could be carried out far more quickly from, say, eighty feet, than from 200. When relatively shallow, the hull and its most vulnerable points, the various hatches, would not already be under intense stress from sea pressure. There were cases of submarine hatches so compressing their rubber seatings, under depth-charging, that the rubber split, the seal was broken, the water gushed in and the only option was to surface, scuttle the submarine and swim for it; there was no stowage space for life rafts. Should the depth-charge be further away from the submarine than the depth-charge was from the surface, as was often the case, the depth-charge's pressure wave, starting to collapse when venting to the atmosphere, would be weakening when it reached the submarine.

There were counter-arguments. The deeper a submarine was, the faster it could go without making propeller noise. But then *Torbay* never used speed when under attack; she played possum, but with one exception: as soon as a depth-charge pattern started to explode, the motor room, without any orders being passed, went half ahead group up for about half a minute, thus giving *Torbay* a boost in the direction she wanted to go. In the hurly-burly of the wake of attacking ships, plus the reverberations of the depth-charges, the sudden short burst of speed was unlikely to be detected.

Had the enemy had a more precise detection system, it

would have been a different story. German U-boats, under attack, used to seek the depths, even 800 feet, to induce errors in British detection and attack methods; in particular, for a time the British had no depth-charges designed for a depth greater than 500 feet. Also some of our colleagues in the Mediterranean were of the 'deep' rather than the 'shallow' school.

In the circumstances, the writer believes that the shallow theory was, in the light of the enemy's equipment and tactics, the better. He followed it in his own submarine, HMS *Upstart*, in the Mediterranean in 1943 and 1944. He is still around, but there must also be a lot of luck in it.

Tony Miers got mild censure for this incident; no part of his patrol orders included attacking destroyers.

That night *Torbay* moved to a position east of Corfu island, off Greece and Albania.

In the early daylight of 4 March a convoy was seen leaving the south end of the Corfu Channel and southbound. *Torbay* gave chase and expended a lot of battery power; but there was no chance of getting within range. Miers decided that a position close south of the Corfu Channel would be better, and *Torbay* moved slowly in that direction.

At 0925, when *Torbay* was still some way from the selected position, the most impressive convoy she had ever seen appeared. It was four large troopships, estimated to range from 15,000 to 8,000 tons, northbound with an escort of three destroyers. Once again came the frustration of not being able sufficiently to close the range, and this time the effort to do so really took the stuffing out of *Torbay*'s batteries. The convoy disappeared into the landlocked waters of the thirty-mile-long Corfu Channel.

Miers pondered. The enemy usually reckoned to be safer by day, when their air cover operated, than by night, when air cover was in those days ineffective. Thus the convoy was likely to anchor in Corfu Roads and to continue to Italy via the north exit from the channel the following day. If *Torbay* could somehow get to Corfu

Roads that night, she might attack by moonlight or at dawn. It was one day after full moon, so there should be reasonable light by night, and sea conditions were glassy calm. Well, how about getting to Corfu Roads? *Torbay* was close to the south entrance to the Channel, but this was twenty miles from the roads, which were less than half that from the north entrance, which would be the more obvious approach route for a marauder. But for that very reason the north entrance was likely to be the more heavily patrolled and/or mined.

Recent experience at Navarin and Suda Bay indicated that controlled minefields and booms and nets might well form part of defences. Things did not look all that promising, particularly since *Torbay* needed several undisturbed hours on the surface in order to charge her batteries.

Miers' plan was to go submerged through the narrow part of the southern entrance, starting at dusk. Once clear of the narrows, *Torbay* would go on the surface to a position east of Corfu Roads; then we would stop and charge batteries; after they were sufficiently restored, *Torbay* would dive and attack by moonlight or at dawn. It would sometimes happen, when Miers expounded his intentions, that the first lieutenant would point out some of the difficulties and dangers, lest these had not been given proper consideration. On this occasion the first lieutenant kept his thoughts to himself; they were: 'Probably we will get in, but the twenty miles to get out, in the face of an alerted enemy, is quite another matter. So what? We are a pawn for a queen, and that is a good trade-off.'

Execution started according to plan, and *Torbay* surfaced a mile and a half off Sivota island when it was dark. At first she went northwards on the motors lest the noise of the diesel engines be heard ashore. Soon after we got under way on the engines, a small merchant vessel was seen approaching from astern; this was, in fact, a blessing in disguise; *Torbay* dived, surfaced a prudent distance behind her, then followed her towards Corfu Roads. A submarine, end on, is a very small target to see in the dark, and it is notorious that the human tendency is to look out ahead rather than astern.

By 2200 *Torbay*, being five miles east of the roads, stopped to charge batteries. The submarine was trimmed right down to present the smallest possible silhouette, and she kept end-on to the moon, which was by then well up and brilliant. At midnight came orders from Alexandria recalling us; after studying the timings Miers commented, 'I was relieved to find that the orders did not conflict with the present operation.'

Just before 0100 on the 5th, a patrol trawler approached and *Torbay* dived. The batteries still wanted quite a lot more, but they had already had about three hours at high charging rates. Miers decided that that was all they could have, because the risk of being seen, if *Torbay* stayed on the surface, was not acceptable. *Torbay* set off submerged across the bay at dead slow speed; this was not only to conserve battery but also in case of any harbour defence Sonar or hydrophones.

At 0235 *Torbay* managed to get a navigational fix by moonlight through the periscope; this was not easy, and it says much for the acumen of David Verschoyle-Campbell. *Torbay* found that she was already in the anchorage, having experienced an unexpectedly strong westerly set – which is another term for current. The disappointment was that, although prominent points of land could be identified through the periscope, ships could not. That meant that there was nothing for it but to wait until dawn, with the consequence that the withdrawal and hopeful escape would have to be in full daylight, which would rule out any chance of a surface dash. In Air Force terms, one would say that *Torbay* stooged slowly around off the anchorage, constantly dodging patrol vessels which were often heard rather than seen.

At 0640 *Torbay* again closed the anchorage; it was getting light, but she had to turn away to avoid being rammed by a patrol vessel. Then came the second and great disappointment. The convoy of troopships was not there; probably they had not stopped off at all but had gone straight on the day before and out through the northern exit. Here one may say that, even if we had guessed this, there was still nothing that *Torbay* could have done to catch them. They were 17- or 20-knotters against *Torbay*'s 14 knots on the surface; but even this would not have been practicable, for, what with constant dives to avoid air patrols, *Torbay* would have been lucky to average about 7 knots. The troopships, being northbound, were probably empty except perhaps for leave parties and 'Blighty' wounded; even so, so long as they were in business, they could go back and forth and continue the build-up that was in due course to drive us back to the lines of El Alamein, when the fleet evacuated Alexandria, and the submarine depot ship *Medway* was sunk by a U-boat; indeed, the biter was bit.

The journey, however, was not entirely in vain; in the anchorage were one destroyer and two supply ships of perhaps 8,000 and 5,000 tons. Just after 0730 two torpedoes were fired at each of the three targets. The supply ships in due course sank, but the torpedoes ran under the destroyer. Miers admitted that, having had two torpedoes set to run specially shallow for the destroyer, in the excitement of the moment he had used them on one of the deeper draught supply ships.

The withdrawal, which the first lieutenant had judged as the most difficult part, turned out to be relatively easy. *Torbay* headed for the southern entrance, deep and at about 4½ knots; this was all that was prudent, bearing in mind that there were at least twenty miles to go, with the battery only some seventy per cent charged. Every thirty minutes we came to periscope depth to fix and to look. We saw patrol vessels milling about the firing-position, aircraft overhead and a destroyer astern. Twice, patrol vessels passed at speed going from south to north. It would seem, that the enemy suspected the anchorage and the 'obvious' northern entrance rather than the much more distant southern entrance; the forty depth-charges heard between 0830 and 1000 were all well astern. Just before *Torbay* reached the southern entrance, a schooner was observed pulling across it, there being no wind to help her; she may have been towing some sort of obstruction, but *Torbay* passed clear ahead of her at 1120. Finally *Torbay* cleared the Corfu Channel at noon on 5 March; she had been inside the enclosed waters for seventeen hours. During this time Miers had no rest, Chapman and Campbell perhaps a couple of hours each in snatches.

Once again the first lieutenant kept his thoughts to himself; they were, 'Tomorrow is my twenty-second birthday; perhaps I shall not spend it in a prisoner-of-war camp after all.' Being taken prisoner at an early stage of what was clearly going to be a long war would have been a frightful bore and a very stern test of character. The idea of being killed, should it cross the mind, passed like a summer cloud; so far as we know, it happens only once, and it is relatively quick.

When out in the open sea, *Torbay* reduced to dead slow speed; the battery was dangerously low, and the first lieutenant, as housekeeper, made it clear that high speed or high jinks were really not on. Thus an anti-submarine trawler, towing a motor launch, was allowed to pass. Later a small schooner was sighted; this was too tempting for Miers, who made towards her to gun her down. However, to the first lieutenant's rescue came a patrolling aircraft, so the schooner also was allowed to pass. Wellington had said, at Waterloo, 'I wish to God Blücher or night would come.' The first lieutenant did not want Blücher and said to himself something like, 'Swiftly walk over the western wave, spirit of night; Out of the misty eastern cave, Where through the daylight long and drear, Thou weavest dreams of love and fear; Speed forth thy flight.'

At length came the blessed, protective dark. *Torbay* surfaced, disconnected both engines from the propellers and put both engines to the task of restoring the batteries – in slang 'getting some amps back in the box'. This meant that *Torbay* was a real sitting duck, since to stop an engine and to get just one propeller shaft connected could take a couple of minutes or more. We had never taken this risk before, nor did we again. It is a matter of balancing risks; a submarine with no electric power is like a car with no gas in the tank; in working order it may be, but it will not work.

Of course, you may not go on charging batteries at maximum permitted rate plus ten per cent indefinitely;

you will else get a disastrous explosion. Thus, after a couple of hours with both engines charging, the first lieutenant reduced the charging rate and offered Miers one engine all to himself.

Torbay had already been recalled and made towards Alexandria; and on 6 March, forty miles west of Cape Skinari on the isle of Zante, she spoke with her sister submarine *Thorn*, passing the latest information about the area she had just vacated. Later in the same day came fresh instructions: *Torbay* and *Thorn* were to rush to the Gulf of Taranto, to try to catch a convoy escorted by three cruisers and an uncertain number of destroyers. *Torbay* arrived at night on 7 March but saw nothing. On the evening of 9 March she was sent close to Messina in Sicily by the toe of Italy, where some cruisers were expected. The position was reached on 10 March in the morning, but once again nothing was seen, and in the evening of that day *Torbay* was for the second time ordered home.

Torbay was on the way home when, at dawn on 12 March, it was seen from the bridge that a torpedo was sticking out from the port forward upper deck (No. 8) tube. A torpedo, when within the tube, is not armed, so that the warhead will not explode from a chance blow, such as the pressure wave of a depth-charge. The warhead had 'whiskers' on its front, and as the torpedo went through the water, the whiskers revolved and drove the detonators down within the primer, which was already within the main explosive of the warhead. Then the torpedo would be armed and ready to explode if it hit anything with its whiskers.

We had no means of knowing whether or not the night passage had turned the whiskers and armed the torpedo. Again, the first lieutenant kept his thoughts to himself; they were: 'That is all we needed.' Off went Tono Kidd, with a helper and a crowbar, to see if he could persuade the torpedo the rest of the way out of the tube; obviously we did not want it back. Kidd could not; being in an unnatural position about one fifth the way out, the torpedo had jammed. The next gambit was to get the sea to help take its weight to help lift it from its jammed position; *Torbay* dived going astern and tried to discharge it by air blast. This was successful at the second attempt.

Moving eastwards, *Torbay* had a look at Benghazi on the 14th and at Apollonia on the 15th, but there was nothing doing. She reached Alexandria on 18 March, having been out for twenty-six days.

Three merchant ships, fifty-five air patrols, nineteen patrol vessels, sixty-four depth-charges.

It is generally held that the Victoria Cross for Tony Miers and other decorations for *Torbay*'s people, including the Distinguished Service Order for Tono Kidd, were in respect of the Corfu operation. This is not quite so. The recommendations for awards were made in respect of *Torbay*'s eighth, ninth and tenth (including Corfu) war patrols. The captain submarines and the Honours and Awards Committees in both Egypt and London singled out the Corfu operation as the one which was 'a calculated act of most conspicuous bravery'.

15 Eleventh Patrol –
Gulf of Patras, Argostoli, Levkas,
Corfu, Adriatic, Taranto, Crete

A patrol 'in the best Torbay *tradition'; the gun's
crew distinguish themselves*

This patrol was from 2 to 24 April 1942.

Once again we had the pleasure of having a United
States submariner with us, Lieutenant R.M. Raymond. He
took a full share, as had Lieutenant-Commander Watkins
USN; and, of course, by this time the United States was at
war. Sadly, Raymond was killed some time later, whilst
first lieutenant of a submarine in the Pacific.

Radar was then known in the Royal Navy as Radio
Direction Finding (RDF), but it is simpler to say 'radar',
which is now such a well-known word. *Torbay* had just
been given a small nodule which was mounted on the
bridge and connected by a lead to a receiver in the wireless
office. If *Torbay* was in the sweep of a radar beam, the
receiver was supposed to give a warning buzz. It did so
twice, in the Patra/Levkas area, on 7 and 8 April; by
coincidence, each time the first lieutenant had the surface
watch. On the first occasion he heard a strange vibration,
then came the report from below; the second time he
heard the vibration and said to the look-outs, 'I expect the
wireless office will report radar'; they did. We were never
able to discover whether or not it really was radar, but it
seems most unlikely.

10th and 11th Patrols 1942

On the 8th *Torbay* passed close to mine-sweepers with a motor anti-submarine boat and an aircraft in company. Somebody must have seen or heard something, since *Torbay* got two bombs and four depth-charges. The navigation lights were broken, but not much else. On the 9th two mine-sweepers were seen; also in sight was a trawler with two smaller craft. *Torbay* came up and sank the rear mine-sweeper by gunfire. By this time our long-time navigating officer, David Verschoyle-Campbell, had switched to have charge of torpedoes and gunnery, so this was his 'first blood'. There was to be another first blood before the end of the patrol. A flying boat appeared and patrolled for some time.

In the darkness of the early morning of the 10th *Torbay* had twice to interrupt battery charging to dive to avoid a destroyer. In the morning of the 11th came a convoy of small craft escorted by two anti-submarine trawlers; these were not torpedo targets, and the odds against the gun were not encouraging, so *Torbay* let them pass. That evening, however, a laden schooner on her own was an easier prey, even though she gallantly tried to ram us. In the general dashing about, Campbell sprained an ankle. *Torbay* then made off to the north for Corfu.

On the 12th *Torbay* got a report of a Libya-bound convoy leaving the Adriatic, so off she went to try to intercept, and a further message ordered her to the Gulf of Taranto when no further opportunity at the convoy was on offer. We did not see the convoy; we did see one merchant ship on the 13th, but it passed well out of range.

By the 15th *Torbay* was off Taranto itself; we spotted a barrage balloon which had come adrift from its moorings and was afloat in the sea; it was riddled with bren-gun fire by Corporal Booth, our embarked soldier folboteer, so that it would not be worth salving. On the 16th *Torbay* had to dive in the early morning because of the approach of an anti-submarine trawler; but the latter did not detect. Later in the day we could see that there were battleships in Taranto harbour, but there was nothing going on to tempt them out. In the afternoon a destroyer left Taranto, and another destroyer escorting two small merchant ships went in; but all passed well out of range. On the 17th *Torbay* was ordered back to her original patrol area, Crete and northwards, and she set off eastwards at dusk.

In the dark of the early morning of the 18th *Torbay* dived to avoid a destroyer which seemed to be patrolling about for no particular purpose. As the light grew, it was seen to be a Calipso class. She did have a purpose: she made off to meet a laden merchant ship bound from the Adriatic to North Africa. A long chase of over half an hour followed, until Miers decided that he could not improve on his rather unfavourable position relative to the target; this was at some two miles range on a very broad track. Two torpedoes were fired on a 150-degree track; both hit. It seemed that the stresses of the months had not impaired Miers' eye or judgement; and, of course, the navigating officer, by now Tony Melville-Ross, had had enough observations to develop an accurate plot of enemy movements. This could not be done in the case of a quick 'snap' attack.

The destroyer put priority on picking up survivors, and her eventual counter-attack of sixteen depth-charges was quite ineffective. Two aircraft prowled about but were unable to do themselves any good.

It was after this attack that Lieutenant Raymond explained to us the United States torpedo-angling system already described in Chapter 6. 'If you had had that, Skipper, you could have got the destroyer as well.' So close is the United States Navy/Royal Navy relationship that, probably, now we have; what about Polaris and Trident?

In the dark of the early morning of the 19th *Torbay* again dived because of the approach of a destroyer. When she had passed, *Torbay* surfaced and saw that there were two merchant ships behind her, but they were all dashing south at an estimated 16 knots, and we could not catch them.

It was just after noon, north of Cape Drepano in Crete, when a German armed petrol-carrier came in sight. She was of some 1,400 tons and was armed with a light AA gun in the bow, and with two larger guns amidships and aft; these were probably 75 millimetre or better – in other words, 3-inch or bigger. Miers decided that it would be appropriate to gun her down rather than try torpedoes. Here it may be said that no eyebrows would have been raised had he just let her go by. There was a snag: David Campbell was still with a sprained ankle and was not sufficiently agile to scamper up the gun tower ladder. Even so, said Miers, Chapman and Campbell must change places, as the first lieutenant's job did not require running about. And so it was done.

The petrol-carrier was steering about west when *Torbay* surfaced abaft her beam and opened fire; the first round was a misfire which was dealt with at once in the summary fashion described earlier; and firing resumed. The enemy replied from her midships gun, and she altered course about 180 degrees until she was on an easterly course. This did not help her gunnery; nor did it help *Torbay*'s. Deflexion, which is aim off to allow for enemy movement across the line of fire, had been set for the enemy going the other way, so our shots were falling out for line. Seeing this, Miers tried two torpedoes but, because of the enemy's continual change of course, these missed. Chapman, after some fruitless spotting corrections, decided to set deflexion zero and start again from scratch. Then we started to hit, whilst they did not; this was just as well, as a submarine could suffer mortal damage from just one hit by a 75-millimetre.

Al Phillips, the gunlayer, Felix Gavin, the trainer, and Corporal Booth on the bridge had seen the flashes and puffs coming from the midships gun, and they did not need to be told to concentrate on that part of the ship. All of a sudden there was an explosion just by the midships gun; when the smoke cleared, it was no longer there; nor, probably, were some of the gun's crew. What remained of the enemy gun's crew, plus some others who emerged from the superstructure amidships, proceeded to run aft with the apparent intention of bringing into action the after gun. However, Miers had all the time been closing the range, so that Booth could see very clearly what was afoot. It might be that, as the enemy people ran aft,

Booth's bullets were uncomfortably close behind. Be that as it may, when they reached the after gun, they did not pause; they preferred to carry straight on and jump into the sea over the stern. This drew roars of applause from *Torbay*'s bridge and gun, and the latter continued firing until the enemy was burning merrily.

By this time the shore batteries of Crete had started to fire, and these included guns of 12-inch calibre north of Suda Bay. *Torbay* dived and made off to the east.

This was Phillips' last gun action of the commission, and probably his best. Also he got in the crack he had been waiting for ever since Chapter 11. As he and the first lieutenant were doing the final check around the gun before diving, he remarked: 'I thought you did very well, sir, for a first time, though I did not take much notice of your spotting corrections; of course, I say this politely.' The resulting bellow of laughter made Miers peer down to see what was happening.

RIP Leslie Alfred Phillips DSM & Bar. Miers and Chapman scattered his ashes off Spithead some thirty years later. The enemy could not out-gun him, but cancer could; as the harbour master's launch, with a padre, the widow, the casket, Miers and Chapman went out of Portsmouth harbour, HMS *Vernon* and HMS *Dolphin* sounded the 'alert'. Said Chapman, 'I bet Phillips is chuckling; they never did it for him when alive.'

The tactics in this action were as described in Chapter 2; but the enemy managed a prompt return fire and got off about ten shots before being silenced, and that was not our idea at all. Well, she was well armed, and probably manned by German naval people or by the German equivalent of the British Royal Fleet Auxiliary. Thus she was alert and keeping a good all-round look-out, and her immediate alteration of course saved her from being hit by *Torbay*'s early shots.

The first lieutenant, as he was to be in charge of the gun, had been given the periscope to have a good look at the target, the better to order, before surfacing, the initial range and deflexion to be set on the guns sights when *Torbay* surfaced. Seeing the enemy armament, he had reservations about taking her on with the gun. But he said nothing. He knew that Miers would want to go out with a bang rather than a whimper; here was a target that *could* be attacked; therefore it *would* be attacked.

Corporal Booth, like all the Special Boat Section, put in his own independent report of activities to Roger Courtney. Booth gave a clear opinion that the attack was 'not a good idea', in view of the enemy's superior armament. Chapman's worry had been the light AA gun rather than the heavier guns; there was no knowing whether our topless turret would keep out that sort of shell. But what German would expect to need light AA just north of Suda Bay in 1942? Middle East Air Forces had not got a strike aircraft that could reach there from Egypt; so the light AA was probably not loaded, or even prepared.

The first lieutenant was not, however, worried at taking on the fire-control task from Campbell. Miers was to comment: 'The first shoot of his life'; well, for real, yes, for practice, no. As a midshipman, Chapman had been range officer in the transmitting station (TS) of a cruiser. The TS, on receiving fall-of-shot reports, ordered range corrections to all 8-inch guns, and that was the range officer's job. In his gunnery course at Whale Island, Portsmouth, Chapman had, for the first time in his life, scored one hundred per cent in two examinations, fire control written and fire control practical. After the practical, the two gunners' mates in charge of operating the synthetic trainer behind the scenes came to Chapman.

'We threw everything at you, but you came back with the right answer without a pause; we have recommended one hundred per cent; where did you learn?'

'Perhaps in a boxing ring.'

Imagine a gun duel between two thin-skinned ships, and imagine the chaos that one exploding shell can cause. Whereas heavily armoured ships, such as battleships, can take a severe pounding and still be in reasonable working order, a thin-skinned ship has no such chance. It follows that he who starts hitting first is almost bound to win. It also follows that the gun control officer must be that word-perfect that his reactions are very fast, like those of a batsman facing a fast bowler. The possibilities of fall of shot have to be one of six: left, right, short, over, hit, not observed. To each there is, at least in principle, an obvious answer; the detail may be a matter of judgement – for example, up 200 yards or up 400 yards? The answer should be instantaneous. *Torbay's* many successes with the gun owed much to the gunlayer and to the trainer, but also to the rapid reactions of the various control officers, Foster, Duncan, Sumption, Campbell, Chapman.

We may finish this post-mortem with an incident when Miers and Chapman took an afternoon off at the races at Alexandria. Seated were Miers, Chapman, Consul-General Heathcote-Smith and Admiral Sir Philip Vian.

Out of the blue said Vian, 'You are a disgusting bully, Miers.'

Tony Miers looked grave; there had been occasions when he could have been accused of bullying. Having let that sink in, Vian continued, 'What makes you think that, with your one little pop-gun, you can take on a ship with three guns?'

Miers did not know of Chapman's gunnery background; he just had faith.

It was about a quarter to one when *Torbay* left the burning petrol-carrier. Soon two motor anti-submarine boats came out from Crete. They were gun and depth-charge armed but had no torpedoes. They approached to within about 1,000 yards, then they took station, one on the beam and one astern; then they would stop, except for the occasional engine movement to maintain position. *Torbay* went down to eighty feet, creeping up to periscope depth from time to time to see if they had gone away. At 1600 they were still there; and so they were at 1800. *Torbay* altered course to the north-east and returned to eighty feet. Said Miers, so that only Chapman could hear, 'We are in the most desperate danger, you know'; then he went to his cabin. What the enemy was doing was a tactic to be employed by Captain F.J. Walker, the famous Atlantic U-boat killer – that is, stay with the submerged enemy until at length she is compelled to come to the surface. The situation as regards *Torbay* was that a considerable amount of battery had been expended in the morning on a fruitless chase of a merchant ship, but otherwise the battery had not been punished, nor had the high-pressure air. At slow speeds, considerable endurance remained.

Chapman pondered. Miers had never said that sort of thing before, not even in Corfu Roads. It came to him that Miers was oppressed by the thought that he had taken the pitcher to the well once too often. There was quite a history of submarines being lost on their last, or almost last, patrol, and this was *Torbay*'s last. *Triumph*, *Upholder* and *Urge* had been so lost. Had he, Miers, for the sake of almost 'cutting a dash' by sinking a relatively insignificant target, courted the loss of his boat, plus losing all his highly experienced crew as dead or prisoners? That would be his unique burden.

It did not seem to Chapman to be as bad as that; he got another officer to take the watch and spoke with Miers. The discussion included that we had the wherewithal to stay dived until midnight or later, so that there was still plenty of time in which to shake them off. However, if we could not shake them off, we should come up in the dark, as stealthily as possible, but with 4-inch and bren-guns ready. If possible, we would creep away on the motors, but if they saw us and opened fire, we should reply with all we had. Admittedly the chances of hitting small, fast targets in the dark with the 4-inch were remote, but at least we should be able to riddle their upper works with bren. Corporal Booth had also a tommy-gun.

But what about shaking them off? They might have judged that we would creep away from the scene of the crime at 2 knots and were doing likewise. This theory had a snag: how could they tell whether we were going east, north, or west? Another possibility was that we were leaving a trail of oil or bubbles. But why should that be? We had not been hit. But if this was so, they would no longer be able to follow the trail once it was dark. Yet another possibility was that they could hear us, even though we were in silent routine and going as slowly as possible. They were not transmitting any underwater signal, but they were known to have good hydrophones, which are listeners only. This theory seemed the best of the bunch. So why not go deeper – 300 feet, if you like, instead of eighty – and see what they make of that. Miers ordered to remain on course and to go to 150 feet.

Chapman resumed the watch and took *Torbay* quietly down. Then he briefed the gunlayer and others as to what they might have to do. Nearly two hours later *Torbay* crept up to periscope depth; there was nothing in sight.

Torbay made off along the north coast of Crete towards the Kaso Strait. There were no further incidents, and she reached Alexandria at dawn on 24 April.

One mine-sweeper, two merchant vessels, one schooner, thirty-seven air patrols, twenty-one patrol vessels, twenty depth-charges and two bombs.

In relation to the final encounter with the armed petrol-carrier, Tony Miers commented: '... the fine shooting and steadiness of the gun's crew, which was exemplary, reflects great credit on the first lieutenant who, in the absence through injury of the third officer, was controlling the first shoot of his life ... and on the gunlayer who has accounted for twenty-one vessels in a year.'

Captain submarines commented: 'So ended a patrol which marks the end of *Torbay*'s activities in the Mediterranean, as she is returning home for refit. The patrol was carried out in the best *Torbay* tradition, all attacks being well planned and brilliantly executed. It will be remembered that *Torbay* arrived on the station just over a year ago, with an almost scratch crew owing to last-minute drafting changes and an immediate operation in the Atlantic. The Commanding Officer had no executive officer over the age of twenty-one and a half, but in spite of this *Torbay* went on from success to success under the bold and determined leadership of Commander Miers. Her record reflects the greatest credit on the Commanding Officer and the ship's company.'

Well, whilst *Torbay* was out on her final patrol, Captain 'Sammy' Raw had been relieved by Captain Philip Ruck-Keene ('Ruckers'), who did not know the story quite so well. At the start the oldest executive officer was twenty-one and sixteen days, and the reason for the scratch crew has been described in Chapter 4.

16   Homeward Bound

In which Torbay *sails home and finds a warm welcome*

After a rest period following her final patrol, *Torbay* was bound, in early May 1942, for Gibraltar and Gosport. It had been suggested that, on passage, *Torbay* should deliver supplies to beleaguered Malta; by this time the Royal Navy had been bombed out of the place; the survivors of the Tenth Submarine Flotilla had gone to Alexandria or Gibraltar; and Malta had not even enough mine-sweepers in action properly to keep clear the approach channel. Miers protested that what *Torbay* could carry would be such a drop in the bucket as not to warrant the risk that *Torbay* would run; he won his point.

It added strength to Miers' representations that the submarine *Olympus* had just been sunk by mines in, or just outside, the swept channel leading from Malta westward. The channel went first south-east, from the harbours, then south, then west past the island of Filfla to the Sicilian Narrows. This was a disaster on the *Thetis* (see Chapter 1) scale; *Olympus* was crammed with people whose submarines had been sunk, or put out of action, in the harbours of Malta; nine or so managed the long swim ashore to report what had happened.

It was also the case that *Torbay* was, for her class, very heavily ballasted with solid pig iron which could be removed only in a dry dock. Thus her carrying-capacity was less than that of most T-class submarines. This point was brought home when *Torbay* sailed from Alexandria for Gibraltar. On this occasion all concerned had everything with them, and there were many heavy metallic items included in their kit. In particular, the stokers, who lived almost right aft, had metal models, some large, some small; for example, most of the wardroom silver plate had been fashioned into submarine brooches for wives and girlfriends. It resulted that *Torbay* was heavy by the stern, as described in Chapter 4; this time the only way to put matters to rights was to discharge, to the sea, 500 gallons of precious fresh water from No. 4 fresh water tank. Since *Torbay* was on a relatively short passage rather than a long patrol, this unusual and drastic measure was acceptable.

A day or so before *Torbay* sailed, the Commander-in-Chief, by now Sir Henry Pridham-Wippell, came to inspect and to say farewell; some minutes later so did Admiral Sir Philip Vian, who commanded the light cruisers. Admiral Vian was recently from his triumph in the Gulf of Sirte when, with four light cruisers and eleven destroyers, he had fought off an Italian force which included a battleship and heavy cruisers.

Torbay was to sail at a late tea-time. It was fine, calm and still; very still. The whole depot ship and the crews of submarines in harbour were on deck, and *Torbay* had on her casing all who could be spared from duty below, stokers, telegraphists, seamen, supply ratings. Captain Ruck-Keene broke the hush with a two-minute speech; then *Torbay* slid slowly astern and away to the cheers of the First and Tenth Submarine Flotillas; *Torbay*'s people returned these cheers with a will. So she proceeded, past a cheering Mediterranean Fleet, until she cleared the boom and disappeared into the dusk in the 'Great Pass' leading out of Alexandria.

The cheering Mediterranean Fleet was not as when *Torbay* had arrived about a year previously: all the battleships and the aircraft-carrier had by now been damaged beyond local repair or, in the case of the battleship *Barham*, sunk; those which had been repaired were busy forming an Eastern Fleet to repel Japanese advances into the Indian Ocean. The largest fleet units

were Admiral Vian's Dido-class ligh
powerful units available were the su
they were losing one of the better ones

The passage to Gibraltar was une
when passing close to Malta by night,
half-starved island still defiantly flingir
Many old friends were met at Gibraltar,
depot ship which *Torbay* had met in Ch
time it was under different management

Thence *Torbay* went past Spain and through the Bay of
Biscay to the English Channel, to rendezvous with an
escort vessel off the Lizard in Cornwall. To the same
rendezvous was also bidden the submarine HMS *Unbeaten*,
ex-Tenth Flotilla. Miers was the senior Commanding
Officer, so *Unbeaten* followed *Torbay*. It was a piquant
touch that *Unbeaten*'s then first lieutenant was a certain
'Bobby' Lambert; he and Chapman had been at St Paul's
School together, had joined the Royal Navy together in
Fountain Lake, Portsmouth, in May 1937, and had been
midshipmen together in China in 1938-9. When they met,
they reminded each other of how they had cut afternoon
school one day to see the film *Lullaby on Broadway* and had
got away with it. Did they but know it, *Lullaby on Broadway*
had overtones of the shape of things to come. The musical
included a jingle:

Broadway babies don't sleep tight,
Until the dawning.
Good night, baby,
Sleep tight,
Milkman's on his way.

It was often the case that the nights, on the surface
charging batteries, would be very disturbed, with alarm
situations developing suddenly at the close visibility
distance. At least by day, with Sonar listening and the
periscope scanning in good Mediterranean visibility, you
were not nearly so likely to be 'jumped' as by night. It
seemed now that once again fortune had smiled: their
survival was, in those early years of the war, against the
odds. This was because the submarines were merely

the strategic game of Churchill and Roosevelt, to
from the Axis the control of North Africa and to use
the launch-pad from which to knock Italy out of the
war.

Thus it was that, passing through the Needles Channel
on a brilliant June morning, with sweet scents coming
from the trees of the Isle of Wight, said Chapman, 'It
seems that we are home; I had not really expected it.'

Said Campbell, 'Nor I.'

Off Spithead *Torbay* hoisted her 'Jolly Roger', with
captured swastika and Italian ensigns beneath. Following
the tradition of conforming to senior officer's actions,
Unbeaten also hoisted her Jolly Roger, and this one too was
impressive. The first to see what was happening was a
civilian-manned dockyard dredger, out dumping spoil;
they cheered themselves hoarse, and two threw their caps
into the sea. Movements of HM ships were secret, but
somehow the buzz had got around, so that Southsea
Castle was black with a cheering throng from Portsmouth
and Southsea. Fort Blockhouse, the Alma Mater of
submarines, just past Southsea Castle but on the Gosport
side, gave a disciplined but roaring welcome. So many of
their brood who had done well had not managed to come
back, so *Torbay* and *Unbeaten* made a welcome change.

In 1797, before the Battle of Cape St Vincent, 'Old
Jervie', later Earl St Vincent, had it pointed out to him that
the Spanish had twenty-seven sail of the line against his
fifteen. He ordered the attack to proceed, saying, 'England
needs a victory.' On 8 June 1942 at least Portsmouth,
Southsea and Gosport saw a badly needed one. Nor was
that the end of it. When the Victoria Cross for Tony Miers
was gazetted, some of what had happened was released
for publication. After the investiture at Buckingham
Palace, attended by those pictured in the plate section, the
entire 1941 crew of *Torbay*, with families and friends,
lunched at the Connaught Rooms. Admiral Sir Max
Horton, then in his closing days as Admiral Submarines
before taking the vital anti-U-boat post of Commander-in-
Chief Western Approaches, came to make a short speech
of welcome and thanks.

During a Warship Week to raise funds to fight the war, *Torbay* had been adopted by the town of Paignton, which is in Torbay, Devonshire; consequently the mayor of Paignton was invited to the Connaught Rooms. The mayor had imagined that the 'do' was an Admiralty-sponsored official event; however, it came out that it was a private venture by Miers. He thought that such was not a good idea and asked for permission to speak; the speech was short but it included, 'Do not worry; Paignton will pay.' It was, clearly, a very good speech.

This was one of many kindnesses showered upon *Torbay*. Some other examples may be mentioned. Chapman's wife was by then a Wren at a naval shore wireless station; she was job-changed to Fort Blockhouse. When *Torbay* was in process of clearing Customs, the coxswain of the Customs launch asked the first lieutenant if there was anything he wanted taken ashore. 'Well, a case of Tio Pepe Sherry would be useful.' It was delivered to the hotel that evening.

Torbay had had trouble at the starters' gate but she came from behind to be with the front runners, and there she stayed. And there she continued for a second commission under Robert Julian ('Rumble') Clutterbuck, and then for a third under Compton Patrick ('Pat') Norman. Let us hope that they may be persuaded to tell their story, if only for the benefit of today's Trafalgar-class nuclear-propelled attack submarine HMS *Torbay*; Tony Miers lived just long enough to see her launched.

Tony Miers lived for a further forty-five years; but it is of interest to note the state of 'The Hard Core' at the end of the commission.

Tony Miers had operations for varicose veins in both legs; he had been too long on his feet; Tono Kidd had much the same problem in a different place; Chapman had to have most of his rotten teeth removed. Stress tends to go for the weak point, and then to exaggerate it; however, nobody went sick until we had got *Torbay* home. Only the immensely strong David Campbell was in good nick.

Immensely strong? Yes, but also a gentleman, though quick with his pistol. There was a time when Miers, Campbell and Chapman were having a discussion, of a sort, in the control room. Of a sudden, Chapman lost patience with Campbell; he stooped down, put his head between his legs and carried him on his shoulders past the wireless office and dumped him without ceremony in the petty officers' bathroom. Miers was astonished; he had not before seen ten stone do that to thirteen. But it is quite easy really, if you have been taught how to do the 'fireman's lift', such as was used a lot in World War I to bring in wounded from No Man's Land. Campbell could have used his muscle to bring matters to a halt, but he was a bit disabled by laughter at the incongruity of the situation.

Epilogue

We go our separate ways, but we don't lose touch

In Chapter 4 we promised to tell the saga of the gear that *Torbay* had left behind when given a 'pierhead jump' to the Mediterranean. This is what happened.

Being in Scotland, in winter, we did not have, either in the submarine nor even in the depot ship, white uniforms; they were at home or in store. Cables and signals from Gibraltar gave instructions to families to pack up the whites and to send them as directed by Admiral Submarines. Admiral Submarines designated superintending naval stores officer (SNSO), Deptford, as the assembly point. Then, since the large submarine *Cachalot* was to sail for Alexandria from Devonport, the Admiral directed SNSO to consign them to Plymouth North Road Station, and he directed *Cachalot* to collect from there before sailing.

An officer from *Cachalot*, with transport, turned up early one morning at Plymouth North Road. After wending his way past fire appliances and a maze of fire hoses, he found a weary group of railway, police and fire officers. They were anxiously watching smouldering ruins, lest a light breeze should cause them again to burst into flame; Plymouth had been heavily blitzed the night before. The officers told *Cachalot* what he could do with *Torbay*'s gear if he could find it; so *Cachalot* had to sail without it.

Astonishingly, *Torbay*'s gear was still intact in the wreckage, and in due course it found its way back to Deptford. Meanwhile, in Alexandria, *Torbay* had had to kit themselves up; you can not survive an Egyptian summer in heavy woollen sweaters and long johns. A financial grant was made, but this was meagre, on the basis that it was just to tide us over whilst our Admiral 'did his best about our gear'. You can not live at the laundry either, so we replaced a full kit largely at own expense.

In due course Deptford found a niche in a convoy going round the Cape of Good Hope to Suez. Thence *Torbay*'s gear came by rail to Alexandria and the depot ship HMS *Medway*. But by this time *Torbay* was at Gibraltar on her way home to Gosport. So *Medway* put the gear, fortunately in a named ship, in a returning convoy, again going round the Cape. *Medway* so advised Captain Submarines at Gosport, and he told *Torbay*.

Meanwhile Chapman and Campbell, in the euphoria of the rather unexpected return home, had brought their wives to the Queen's Hotel, Southsea. This turned out to be more expensive than foreseen. The position was reached when, although they paid from time to time something on account, they could not settle the whole – that is, except by a moonlight flit, which was hardly becoming to an officer.

Then daily situation reports showed that the ship with *Torbay*'s gear had been torpedoed and sunk off Freetown. 'Ho, Ho,' said Tony Miers. 'Now we can claim full compensation.' Thus Chapman and Campbell were able to settle their accounts, leave and lodge more frugally thereafter.

A lot of people, as well as our Admiral, had done their best about our gear, but it took a U-boat to hit the jackpot. Said Chapman to Campbell, 'Should we not sing at least the first verse of *Hymns Ancient and Modern*, number 373? "God moves in a mysterious way, His wonders to perform".'

After some time at Gosport, Devonport had a refitting berth available for *Torbay*, and so she was to sail thither. Ever mindful of his duty to train his young people, Tony Miers told Chapman to arrange the trip and to take command during it. He would be there, in his cabin, but he would interfere only if asked. Thus in his cabin he stayed, except to come up to watch Chapman take *Torbay* past Drake's Island, then to the Devonport Dockyard area, then into a dockyard basin at right angles to a sluicing River Tamar.

There were but few, apart from Miers, who would have exercised such discretion and trust. In 1942 enemy air attack by day in the English Channel was not out of the ordinàry; by night E-boats and even destroyers were at large. German destroyers, later on, sank the cruiser HMS *Charybdis* in the Channel; in 1944 German E-boats based on the Channel Islands inflicted severe casualties on an American force doing a D-Day rehearsal off Slapton Sands in Devonshire. Had *Torbay* come under attack, it was understood that Miers would resume control; but he might not have been able to reach the bridge before important decisions had to be taken – for example, to dive or not to dive. Had the decision been to dive, he would have been brushed aside in the rush of at least five people coming down the conning tower ladder; on this thing there is no possibility for two-way traffic. In the dark hours, Chapman was on the bridge chart table, as Miers had been in the Mediterranean. Another point is that, coming from the almost tideless waters of the Mediterranean, manoeuvring into a narrow hole across a roaring ebb tide was an experience in which we were hardly in practice.

Once safely into the dockyard, *Torbay* was honoured by a visit by the Commander-in-Chief, Admiral Sir Charles Forbes; Miers had been on his staff at the beginning of the war, when Sir Charles had been Commander-in-Chief Home Fleet.

The health problems of the 'Hard Core' have been outlined in Chapter 15, as have some kindnesses. Now that *Torbay* was out of action in refit, something could be done about health. Tony Miers was dealt with at a London teaching hospital; he emerged in a wheelchair, to stay at 'The Rag' in Pall Mall. There the club staff fussed about their VC like a lot of wet hens; Miers asked Chapman to lunch.

In the meantime, Chapman had been asked to call on Sir Max Horton, Admiral Submarines. Sir Max always liked to interview those to whom it was proposed to entrust command of one of his submarines, before they did the Commanding Officers' qualifying course.

Said Sir Max, 'You are not very fit; what are we to do, sort you out and then send you to the course, or the other way round?'

Said Chapman, 'I can carry on to the course, sir, and get sorted out later.'

'I thought that you would say that; but it will not be so; there is a car outside to take you to see my friend Mr Bridgland at the London Clinic; so get on your way.'

Thus Chapman was dealt with by Dr George Exner, at the London Clinic, and at his dental surgery in Wimpole Street. It seemed that high-faluting doctors were 'misters' and not 'doctors', on the other hand, the eminent dentist George Exner was a doctor.

Later Dr Exner took hot wax impressions of Chapman's jaw, with a view to designing dentures; but he left the wax in just a trifle too long, so that it took all his strength to yank the plates out. Chapman was a little astonished that what remained of his teeth were still in place, and in the meantime he had had a fit of the giggles.

Said Exner, 'What was so bloody funny? That was careless.'

'Well, sir, I was thinking what a good advertisement it would be for you if I walked down Wimpole Street looking like a duck-billed platypus.'

Somebody in the Admiralty looked up the 'Rule Book'. It seemed that, since Chapman's teeth had not actually been shot out by the enemy, he should pay for his dentures. Sir Max Horton smote this back over the bowler's head for such a soaring six that it had ice on it when the ball came down.

At lunch at The Rag, Tony Miers gave Chapman his valedictory report, known in the Royal Navy as a 'flimsy', because it was on a very small and thin piece of paper. Miers had to write small because there were several things he wished to say, so the flimsy took a bit of reading. Chapman got as far as '... has been a brilliantly successful first lieutenant, and handled the ship with remarkable skill. Loyal, trustworthy and reliable to an exceptional degree ...', then he looked over his left shoulder, then over the right.

'Why do you do that?'

'Well, sir, I was wondering whether to have my jacket altered to accommodate folded wings.'

'You always were an impertinent so-and-so, but there is no room on the flimsy to say so.'

Well, had there been summer storms? Yes, there had been; any contemporary would know this, but summer storms they were. Two disparate characters, even though both had the same aim, would have areas of disagreement. Be that as it may, the friendship lasted until death us temporarily parted.

Of *Torbay*'s crew a nucleus stayed on for the next commission, but the greater part of this seasoned crew split off to provide a leaven of experience for new or refitted submarines.

Tony Miers went on a speaking-tour in the United States. To his chagrin, his captured German and Italian ensigns were stolen; well, that's life. Then he went to Hawaii to join the staff of the United States Commander-in-Chief Pacific. Here his diagnosis of the fact that American torpedoes suffered a malfunction was of considerable importance to our ally. Once they had accepted the unpalatable truth, the Americans soon took the necessary steps, but in the meantime some targets had got away in a manner most frustrating to the attacking submarines. What had been happening was that, at certain angles of incidence torpedo-target, the firing mechanism had been crushed before it could operate. Miers' report and analysis were for the chief of staff but as a matter of courtesy he dropped a copy, at the same time, on the desk of the staff torpedo officer.

Seeing Miers at lunch, the staff officer remarked, 'I thought you were a friend of mine.'

'I hope I am, but is that quite the point?'

Pride, even professional pride, has its dangers.

David Verschoyle-Campbell took over as first lieutenant, whilst Chapman went to the command course. Campbell did not stay long before he too was called for command. Thus it happened that the two met again in Scotland in mid 1943 commanding the new submarines *Upstart* and *Stonehenge*. They did not meet after that: *Upstart* went to the Mediterranean, and *Stonehenge* was lost with all hands in the Far East in 1944; so was Bobby Lambert, commanding his submarine, but in his case he was torpedoed by a U-boat near Freetown.

The loss, at a late stage in the war, of two such close colleagues as David Verschoyle-Campbell and Bobby Lambert made a deep impression on Chapman. His friends had survived the heat and burden of the day, when Allied submarines faced appalling odds and suffered heavy losses, only to fall victims during a period when the enemy was greatly weakened and our submarine losses were few and far between. The matter led to the self-addressed question. 'Why am I still around?' Said the padre at Gibraltar, 'Probably it is because you still have a lot to learn.' It is no good moping. Remember Kipling's 'If':

If you can meet with triumph and disaster
And treat those two impostors just the same; ...
You'll be a man, my son.

Lieutenant Kidd, the engineer officer, went to the new submarine *Tantalus*, being built at Barrow-in-Furness. There he found Chapman building *Upstart*. By strange coincidence, their paths were again to cross: in 1951 Tony Miers was commanding the First Submarine Squadron in Malta, with Lieutenant-Commander Chapman as his senior submarine officer. Across the creeks was Commander Kidd as chief engineer of a destroyer squadron. Their lives, though full and varied with manifold peace-time duties, were not as fraught as in the days of *Torbay*'s living up to her motto '*Penetrabo*'.

There should be, so they say, some love interest somewhere in a book. Well, in 1945 Tono Kidd married Mildred, whom he had met as a Wren in Alexandria in

1942. Tony Miers, when he had finished at Hawaii, went as Commander Submarines to a flotilla based in Australia; here he met his match in Patricia Miller, to whom as Lady Miers, this tale is dedicated.

In 1985, at the Memorial Service for Sir Tony Miers in the cathedral of St George, Southwark, His Royal Highness The Duke of Edinburgh was represented by Admiral of the Fleet Sir John Fieldhouse, Chief of the Defence Staff and a submariner. The Board of Admiralty were there. It took about forty minutes for those present to file past Lady Miers, her daughter Angela and son John. Meanwhile the former first lieutenant, illegally, had opened a side door for the benefit of those bursting to get out for a pee. Nor did the first lieutenant leave until he had checked that there were no somnolents still collapsed under pews; that had been his standing duty when Tony Miers gave a party.

Afterword:
The Miers Controversy

In 1989, when this book had been virtually completed, a story burst in the national and some local press and radio. It was to the effect that *Torbay*'s actions, on the 4 and 9 July 1941, amounted to war crimes.

We know who inspired the story, but we do not know why. The writer's opinion, for what it may be worth, is that there is more of a resemblance to a publicity stunt than to an unburdening of conscience. He who inspired the story was in home waters on the date in question, and had known of the matters for some years.

The principal actors in the drama, Sir Andrew Cunningham, the Commander-in-Chief, Sir Sidney Raw, then Captain Submarines in Alexandria, Sir Anthony Miers, then *Torbay*'s Commanding Officer, and David Verschoyle-Campbell, *Torbay*'s officer of the watch at the time, are long since dead. We cannot know what advice, which almost certainly would have been verbal, was given to Miers in the matter of whether or not to take prisoners. But it *is* known that neither Sir Andrew nor Sir Sidney demurred at what was done. It is also the case that nobody would contemplate having a bunch of fanatical Nazis at large in a submarine, where there is no secure place to put them. *Torbay* took but one enemy soldier back to Alexandria (see Chapter 13); he was an Austrian, and a deserter vouched for as such by the Cretan Resistance.

The writer does know of various moods of Sir Andrew Cunningham. During the Battle of Crete and the evacuation, when ships were being sunk and damaged like ninepins, his general signal to the Fleet included the words, 'We must not let the Army down.' To his staff he remarked, 'It takes five years to build a ship, and five hundred to build a tradition.' Nearly two years later, when Germans sought to escape by sea from the Tunisian tip, he signalled to the Fleet, 'Sink, burn, and destroy. Let nothing pass.' (See Churchill, *The Second World War*, Vol. 4, Book II, p. 626.) There is nothing in that about taking prisoners.

The general situation following the Battle of Crete has been described in Chapters 5 and 6, and there is, in Chapter 7, a description of the rescue of 130 Commonwealth troops from Crete. Also we have available, in the Public Record Office, *Torbay*'s related official reports; these are relatively brief as they always were. What may one add to these? It was forty-eight years ago, and some of those who were there have come up with widely divergent versions; here it is important to differentiate between 'eyewitness' and 'hearsay'; also one must accept that, after 48 years, even 'eyewitness' may be unreliable.

Be the foregoing as it may, the following are believed to be facts beyond all reasonable doubt:

The Germans on 9 July were treacherous – they were trying to use arms after having called surrender; Bremner and Campbell shot one each for that reason. The Germans did seek to decamp in a large and seaworthy rubber boat, not unlike that used by *Torbay* in Chapter 13. The ambient and calm conditions were such that the Germans could easily have reached safety on Antikithera Island.

According to the official report, and to German reports, the Germans were killed in their rubber boat. The writer heard the Lewis gun firing, but he does not know who fired it, nor has anyone come forward so to say.

What follows is the writer's opinion, bearing in mind that it was not 'eyewitness'. It is unlikely that German soldiers of this type would be unarmed, even though one witness (though not of the shooting) has said that he had disarmed them and had paraded them on the casing (whereas another witness in a prime position to see says that no such thing ever happened.

Side-arms are easy to conceal, and the Germans used

lollipop-shaped grenades on a stick; this is unlike the British Mills hand-grenade which is like a cricket ball; it was easy to have the stick in the waistband and the business end inside the trousers.

The controversy relates in the main to the last target of the gun action before dawn on 9 July; the caique had been dealt with by demolition charges; thus probably the 4-inch gun's crew had been stood down; this would reduce dramatically the number of men in a position to see; only the bridge would be manned, with captain, officer of the watch, and four look-outs; but look-outs were expressly forbidden to look other than in their own 90-degree sector (Chapter 2); that would leave just Miers, Campbell, and one other (or two if yet another pulled the trigger) in a position to see.

Hardly will one find exact parallels in war, but there are comparable circumstances. See, for example General Alexander's report in Churchill's *The Second World War*, Vol. 4, Book II, p. 622: '... fifty men of the Hermann Goering Division had just surrendered, when one of them persuaded them to take up arms again, and the whole party started fighting and had to be shot to a man.'

Plus ça change? The German 11th Air Corps were also Goering's pets.

Technical Glossary

Abaft	Relative to some other object or position, towards the stern
Aft	At or towards the stern
AIV	Automatic inboard venting to allow water to enter torpedo tube and AIV tank to compensate for weight-loss when a torpedo is discharged
Amidships	In the middle
Anvil	Code-name for Allied landings in the South of France, August 1944
Asdic (also Sonar)	Active or passive underwater detection device
Athwartships	From one side to the other, at right angles to the sides
Axis	The name given to the German and Italian alliance (Berlin/Rome Axis)
Ballast tanks	Main or auxiliary, flooded or emptied as necessary
Ballast pumps	To flood or pump out auxiliary ballast tanks
Batteries	Three in all, each of 112 cells, 240 volts
Boat	Colloquial for 'submarine'
Bren-gun	A light machine-gun
Bubble	Shows fore-and-aft or side-to-side attitude of a submarine
Cant	Italian patrol aircraft
Casing	Perforated free-flooding platform on top of the pressure hull
Charts	Nautical maps

Conning tower	Held the bridge structure of a submarine; it had upper and lower hatches
Counter-weight	Fitted to upper hatches of conning- and gun towers
Davis escape apparatus	Used to escape from sunken submarines
Depth-charges	Sinking explosives used extensively in World War II
Depth-gauge	Showed waterline depth of a submarine ('keel depth' is now used)
Detonator	'Married' with the primer when a torpedo is armed to explode
Dog watches	Two watches, each of two hours, between 1600 and 2000
DSC	Distinguished Service Cross, a decoration for gallantry in naval service by officers
DSM	Distinguished Service Medal; as DSC but for ratings
DSO	Distinguished Service Order, a high award for gallantry common to all the Armed Forces
Felucca	Pulling and sailing craft of the Middle East
Focke Wulf	German long-range reconnaissance aircraft
Four-inch quick-firing gun	Fires a shell of diameter 4 inches
Giraud	French general prominent in North African affairs in 1943 and later
Goeben and *Breslau*	German battle-cruiser and light cruiser respectively which nudged Turkey into war against Russia in October 1914
Gun tower	Led from interior of the submarine to the gun platform; it had upper and lower hatches
Haul	Pull or heave in

HE	Hydrophone effect caused by the noise of moving ships' propellers and machinery
HO	'Hostilities only' – people who had volunteered or had been conscripted only for the duration of hostilities
Hydrophones	Sensitive underwater listening-devices
Hydroplanes	Used by submarines like fishes' fins
Jolly Roger	'Pirate flag' denoting successful actions
Kingston valves	Telemotor-operated sea inlets at the bottom of 'A', 'Q' and 'Z' auxiliary ballast tanks
Klaxon horns	Deafening noises used for emergency orders
Layers	Bodies of water of different temperature and/or salinity
Lid	Slang for 'hatch'
Luftwaffe	German Air Force
Macchi	Italian patrol aircraft
Main line	Pump/flood system connecting auxiliary ballast tanks
Main motors	Electrically driven motive power of a submarine
Molotov	Stalin's Foreign Minister
Net-cutter	Knife-edge blade fitted on the bow of a submarine
On the swing	Firing torpedoes with the ship's head moving, not steady
Oscillator	The primary part of an Asdic or Sonar set
Periscope	Optical tube raised so that a submerged submarine can see
Pressure hull	The pressure-tight part of a submarine
Primer	Small explosive charge used to detonate the main warhead

Pyrotechnic	Like fireworks
Ribbentrop	Hitler's Foreign Minister
Rommel	German general leading the German Afrika Korps in North Africa and later in command of the area of the Allied landings in Normandy in 1944
Saddle tanks	Main ballast tanks external to the pressure hull and looking like blisters on the same
Scharnhorst and *Gneisenau*	Fast, well-armed and armoured German battle cruisers
Snort mast	Hollow tube raised to allow diesel engines to draw in air
Sonar	See Asdic
Sonobuoys	Devices dropped by aircraft to detect submarines
Sumps	Drain down recesses at the bottom of battery tanks
Telemotor system	Operated valves and machinery by remote control
Thetis	Submarine sunk in Liverpool Bay by accident in June 1939; she was raised and renamed *Thunderbolt*
Thunderbolt	See *Thetis*
Tommy-gun	A small sub-machine gun hand-held
Trim	The balance of a submarine
Trot boat	A naval ferry service
TS	Transmitting station controlling gunfire in surface ships
Veer	Let out
Vent	In the top of ballast tanks to admit or release air
Vichy French	The Government of the as-yet-unoccupied part of France
Victoria Cross	The highest British award for gallantry in action
Warhead	The front of a torpedo containing the main explosive

Watch	In normal parlance means people on duty at sea or in harbour; but in the context of mines (sea mines) means that the mine is keeping its pre-set depth
Working up	Exercises and drills to test all equipment and train personnel for the jobs they may have to do
Yawing	Being thrown off course by a following sea or wind

Technical Appendix (ref. p.51)

To discard, as 'Non possumus', such an obvious focal-point at the entrance to the Dardanelles, at that stage of the war, was weak rather than chicken. Had *Torbay* not been close to, she might have found *Alberta* and *Giuseppina Ghiradi* passing out of range; indeed, she might not even have seen them. Chapter 5 says, 'Flooding five tons in was quick enough.' That is shorthand for the general reader; in fact, conventional means of flooding were either unsuitable or not quick enough.

Imagine a 300-foot-long submarine with her midships control-room depth-gauges showing a waterline depth of fifty feet. Also she has a bow-down angle of about 10 degrees as she tries to punch into the 'feather bed'. At this stage her periscope standards will be at about thirty feet and her stern at about twenty-five feet depth. This is the worst of all worlds. The submarine cannot see to dodge, yet she is vulnerable to being struck by a deep-draught vessel such as a loaded tanker.

Torbay's auxiliary ballast tanks included 'A' right forward and 'Z' right aft. These had telemotor-operated Kingston valves and outboard vents direct to the sea, as well as the usual inboard vents and pump and flood connections to the 'main line'. This latter was a system to which all auxiliary ballast tanks were connected. Also there were 'H', 'O' and 'M' tanks respectively between

midships and forward, midships and between midships
and aft. These had main line connections only. There was
also the quick diving tank 'Q'. This was forward of
midships, deliberately so as to help the submarine down
in a hurry; but it was supposed to be flooded and almost
immediately emptied, else the submarine assumed a
permanent and unwanted bow-down angle.

Taking in five tons using 'Q' was thus unsuitable.
Flooding some or all of 'H', 'O' and 'M' via the main line
was too slow. The solution was to use 'A' and 'Z' together;
open the Kingston valves and the inboard vents; if that
still seemed not to get things moving, open also the
outboard vents. This last measure would mean making a
kerfuffle of bubbles on the surface; but better that than to
'hang' around fifty feet.

In fact, *Torbay* used the Kingston valves and both
inboard and outboard vents each time she needed to go
deep off the Dardanelles in a hurry. Down through the
feather bed she went with no delay. The method had not
been taught in Submarine School.

Geographical Glossary

Adriatic	Sea between Italy and Yugoslavia
Aegean	Sea between Greece and Turkey
Alam Halfa	Egypt, sixty miles west of Alexandria
Alamein	As Alam Halfa
Alexandria	Egypt, 130 miles west of the Suez Canal
Algiers	Capital city of Algeria, then French North Africa
Andros	Island in the central Aegean
Antikithera	Small island twenty miles north-west of Crete
Apollonia	Libya, 180 miles west of Egypt
Argostoli	Harbour in the isle of Cephalonia, west of Greece
Barrow-in-Furness	Lancashire, main element of Vickers Armstrong
Baghdad	Capital city of Iraq
Bay of Biscay	West of France and north of Spain
Beda Littoria	Libya, inland from Zaviet el Hamama
Beirut	Capital city of the Lebanon
Benghazi	Libya, near the eastern end of the Gulf of Sirte
Black Sea	Large sea bordering the Soviet Union, Turkey and other countries
Bonifacio Strait	Between Corsica and Sardinia
Bosphorus	Narrow strait leading from the Black Sea to the Sea of Marmara

Cairo	Capital of Egypt
Campbeltown	Scotland, near south tip of Argyll
Candia	Town in central Crete
Capes:	
Drepano	Crete, close east of Suda Bay
Dukato	Isle of Levkas, off western Greece
Helles	Turkey, at entrance to the Dardanelles
Malea	Greece, in southern Peloponnese
Skinari	Isle of Zante, off western Greece
Carlisle	Cumberland
Caucasus	Mountainous area of southern Russia, bordering Turkey and Iran (Persia)
Cephalonia	Isle off the Gulf of Patras, western Greece
Ceylon	Large island off the southern tip of India, now Sri Lanka
Chatham	Kent, on the River Medway
Cirene	Libya, twelve miles south-west of Zaviet el Hamama
Clyde	Scotland, area of lochs and islands west of Glasgow
Coral Sea	North-east of northern Australia
Corinth Canal	Between northern Greece and the Peloponnese
Corfu	Island west of Greece and Albania
Crete	Large island at the south of the Aegean Sea
Cyrenaica	Libya, west of Egypt; the Senussi Arabs were its inhabitants
Dardanelles	The strait leading from the Sea of Marmara to the Mediterranean
Derna	Libya, thirty miles east of Ras Hilal
Devonport	Adjoins Plymouth, Devonshire
Doro Channel	Aegean Sea, between isles of Andros and Euboea
Drake's Island	In Plymouth Sound, Devonshire
Dunoon	In the Holy Loch of the Clyde, q.v.
Durban	In south-east Africa

El Alamein	Egypt, sixty miles west of Alexandria
Euboea	Island in the Aegean Sea very close to the Greek mainland
Falmouth	In Cornwall
Filfla	Small island off south-eastern Malta
Foggia	In southern Italy
Fort Blockhouse	Submarine HQ and base in Gosport, Hampshire
Freetown	Sierra Leone, West Africa
Gibraltar	British colony on the southern tip of Spain
Gosport	Opposite Portsmouth, Hampshire
Greenock	Scotland, in the Clyde, q.v.
Gulf of Athens	Eastern Greece
Holy Loch	In the Clyde, west of Glasgow
Imbros	Island fifteen miles north-east of the Dardanelles
Iran (Persia)	Between the Soviet Union and the Persian Gulf, and next to Iraq
Iraq	At the head of the Persian Gulf
Kaso Strait	Aegean Sea, between eastern Crete and Kaso island
Kithera	Island ten miles south-west of Cape Malea
Kithera Channel	North-west of Crete
La Maddalena	Island in the Bonifacio Strait between Sardinia and Corsica
Lebanon	Country between Syria and Israel
Levkas	Island off western Greece, north of Cephalonia
Loch Long	A long loch in the Clyde, leading almost to Loch Lomond
Madagascar	Large island east of the southern tip of Africa
Malta	British colony in the central Mediterranean
Marmara	A small sea between the Black Sea and the Mediterranean

Marseilles	A large port in southern France
Messina	Sicily, opposite the toe of Italy
Methoni	In the south-west Peloponnese, Greece
Milos	Aegean island about seventy miles north of Crete
Mitylene	Aegean island off the Turkish coast
Montreux	Switzerland; the Montreux Convention was an international agreement governing movement of shipping through the Dardanelles
Mull	Island in the Western Isles of Scotland, near Oban
Mykoni	Island in the central Aegean Sea
Narvik	Port in north Norway
Navarin	Harbour in the south-western corner of the Peloponnese, Greece
New South Wales	Province in south-east Australia
North Cape	In northern Norway
Paignton	Town in Torbay, South Devonshire
Patras	Gulf between the Peloponnese and northern Greece
Paximadia	Island off the south-west of Crete
Peloponnese	The southern part of Greece
Phalonnera	Small island north-west of Milos island in the Aegean
Piraeus	The port of Athens, Greece
Port Said	Egypt, north end of the Suez Canal
Port Vendres	South-eastern France, close to the frontier with Spain
Preveli	Monastery in south-western Crete
Pylos	Island off Navarin in the Peloponnese, Greece
Rabbit Island	Close south of the Dardanelles, Turkey
Ras el Hamama	As Zaviet el Hamama

Ras Hilal	Ten miles east of Apollonia, Libya
River Plate	In Uruguay, South America
Rhodes	Large island in the Dodecanese, east of Crete
St Vincent	Cape in south-western Spain
San Giorgio	Island near the mouth of the Gulf of Athens
Sardinia	Large island between Italy and Spain
Scapa Flow	Large fleet anchorage in the Orkneys, Scotland
Sheerness	At the mouth of the River Medway, Kent
Sicily	Large island east of the toe of Italy
Sirte	Gulf in the Eastern Mediterranean bordering Libya and Tripolitania
Sivota	Island in the south entrance to the Corfu Channel
Sphakia	In south-west Crete
Spithead	In the Solent, north of the Isle of Wight
Suda Bay	Large anchorage on western Crete's north coast
Suez Canal	Joins the Mediterranean to the Red Sea; designed by Ferdinand de Lesseps
Syria	Eastern Mediterranean country north of Israel
Tamar	River running through Devonport, Devonshire
Taranto	Gulf and large naval base in southern Italy
Tehran	Capital city of Iran (Persia)
Thermia Channel	Aegean Sea, between isles of Thermia and Zea
Tobermory	In the Isle of Mull, Western Isles, Scotland
Trafalgar	Off southern Spain; Nelson died here
Triaklisia	In south-eastern Crete

Vancouver	City on the west coast of Canada
Zante	Island west of the Peloponnese
Zaviet el Hamama	Libya, seventeen miles west of Apollonia
Zea Channel	In the Aegean between the Greek mainland and Zea island

Index

Index